The
Secret of
Divine
Civilization

'Abdu'l-Bahá

The Secret of Divine Civilization

translated from the Persian
by
Marzieh Gail
in consultation with
Ali-Kuli Khan

Bahá'í
PUBLISHING

Bahá'í Publishing
401 Greenleaf Avenue, Wilmette, Illinois 60091-2844

Copyright © 2007 by the National Spiritual Assembly
of the Bahá'ís of the United States

19   18   17   16   4   3   2

Cataloging-in-Publication Data
'Abdu'l-Bahá, 1844–1921.
    [Asrar al-ghaybiyah li-asbab al-madaniyah. English]
    The secret of divine civilization / 'Abdu'l-Bahá; trans-
lated from the Persian by
    Marzieh Gail in consultation with Ali-Kuli Khan. — 1st
Bahá'í Pub. ed.
        p. cm.
    Includes index.
    ISBN-13: 978-1-931847-51-3 (alk. paper)
    ISBN-10: 1-931847-51-7 (alk. paper)
    1. Bahai Faith. 2. Civilization. 3. Iran. I. Gail,
Marzieh. II. Khan, Ali-Kuli. III. Title.

BP363.A9413 2007
294.9'3824—dc22

                                        2007060815

Contents

Introduction vii

The Secret of Divine Civilization 3

Glossary 151

Index 161

Introduction

Since its beginning in Persia in the mid-nineteenth century, the Bahá'í Faith has spread to virtually every corner of the earth. As members of the youngest of the world's independent religions, Bahá'ís today make up what may well be the most ethnically and culturally diverse organized association of people on the planet. The growth of the Bahá'í Faith has been fueled by a body of teachings that its followers regard as the Revelation of God's guidance for the collective coming-of-age of humankind: the oneness of the human race, the oneness of the world's religions as the principal civilizing force in history, and the imperative challenge facing the earth's inhabitants to construct a global society based on principles of unity and justice.

One of the Faith's striking features is that it owes its origin to the labors of two successive founding Prophets: the Báb and Bahá'u'lláh. As the former explained, His mission was to prepare the way for "Him Whom God shall make manifest," the Manifestation of God awaited by the followers of all faiths. During the course of successive waves of persecution that followed this announcement and that claimed the lives of the Báb and several thousand of His followers, Bahá'u'lláh declared Himself to be the fulfillment of the Divine promise. It is thus the voluminous body of the latter's writings that constitutes the main corpus of Bahá'í scripture. However, in His Will and Testament, Bahá'u'lláh appointed His eldest son, 'Abdu'l-Bahá, as the Center of His Covenant and the interpreter of His writings. Thus the writings of 'Abdu'l-Bahá are among the sacred scriptures of the Bahá'í Faith.

The Secret of Divine Civilization is one of many works written by 'Abdu'l-Bahá. It is a treatise that was addressed to the rulers and the people of Persia (now known as Iran) in 1875. The original Persian text of *The Secret of Divine Civilization* was lithographed in Bombay in 1882, and the first English translation was published in London in 1910. It was later published in Chicago in

1918 under the title *Mysterious Forces of Civilization*. The current volume includes a new introduction, a glossary, and some additional notes.

Although the message of *The Secret of Divine Civilization* was penned more than a century ago, its enduring relevance will be readily apparent to readers. The rapid spread of the Bahá'í Faith around the world today and the consequent rising interest in its primary texts have prompted the decision to make available this edition, which we are happy to offer.

THE NATIONAL SPIRITUAL ASSEMBLY OF
THE BAHÁ'ÍS OF THE UNITED STATES

The
Secret of
Divine
Civilization

*In the Name of God the Clement,
the Merciful*

Praise and thanksgiving be unto Provi- 1
dence that out of all the realities in
existence He has chosen the reality of
man and has honored it with intellect and wisdom, the two most luminous lights in either
world. Through the agency of this great
endowment, He has in every epoch cast on the
mirror of creation new and wonderful con-
figurations. If we look objectively upon the world
of being, it will become apparent that from age
to age, the temple of existence has continually been embellished with a fresh grace, and
distinguished with an ever-varying splendor,
deriving from wisdom and the power of thought.

This supreme emblem of God stands first in 2
the order of creation and first in rank, taking pre-
cedence over all created things. Witness to it is
the Holy Tradition, "Before all else, God created

3

the mind." From the dawn of creation, it was made to be revealed in the temple of man.

3 Sanctified is the Lord, Who with the dazzling rays of this strange, heavenly power has made our world of darkness the envy of the worlds of light: "And the earth shall shine with the light of her Lord."[1] and exalted is He, Who has caused the nature of man to be the dayspring of this boundless grace: "The God of mercy hath taught the Qur'án, hath created man, hath taught him articulate speech."[2]

4 O ye that have minds to know! Raise up your suppliant hands to the heaven of the one God, and humble yourselves and be lowly before Him, and thank Him for this supreme endowment, and implore Him to succor us until, in this present age, godlike impulses may radiate from the conscience of mankind, and this divinely kindled fire which has been entrusted to the human heart may never die away.

5 Consider carefully: all these highly varied phenomena, these concepts, this knowledge, these

1. Qur'án 39:69.
2. Qur'án 55:1–3.

technical procedures and philosophical systems, these sciences, arts, industries and inventions—all are emanations of the human mind. Whatever people has ventured deeper into this shoreless sea, has come to excel the rest. The happiness and pride of a nation consist in this, that it should shine out like the sun in the high heaven of knowledge. "Shall they who have knowledge and they who have it not, be treated alike?"[3] And the honor and distinction of the individual consist in this, that he among all the world's multitudes should become a source of social good. Is any larger bounty conceivable than this, that an individual, looking within himself, should find that by the confirming grace of God he has become the cause of peace and well-being, of happiness and advantage to his fellow men? No, by the one true God, there is no greater bliss, no more complete delight.

---

3. Qur'án 39:12.

6 How long shall we drift on the wings of passion and vain desire; how long shall we spend our days like barbarians in the depths of ignorance and abomination? God has given us eyes, that we may look about us at the world, and lay hold of whatsoever will further civilization and the arts of living. He has given us ears, that we may hear and profit by the wisdom of scholars and philosophers and arise to promote and practice it. Senses and faculties have been bestowed upon us, to be devoted to the service of the general good; so that we, distinguished above all other forms of life for perceptiveness and reason, should labor at all times and along all lines, whether the occasion be great or small, ordinary or extraordinary, until all mankind are safely gathered into the impregnable stronghold of knowledge. We should continually be establishing new bases for human happiness and creating and promoting new instrumentalities toward this end. How excellent, how honorable is man if he arises to fulfill his responsibilities; how wretched and contemptible, if he shuts his eyes to the welfare of society and wastes his precious life in pursuing his own selfish interests and personal advantages. Supreme happiness is

man's, and he beholds the signs of God in the world and in the human soul, if he urges on the steed of high endeavor in the arena of civilization and justice. "We will surely show them Our signs in the world and within themselves."[4]

And this is man's uttermost wretchedness: that he should live inert, apathetic, dull, involved only with his own base appetites. When he is thus, he has his being in the deepest ignorance and savagery, sinking lower than the brute beasts. "They are like the brutes: Yea, they go more astray . . . For the vilest beasts in God's sight, are the deaf, the dumb, who understand not."[5]   7

We must now highly resolve to arise and lay hold of all those instrumentalities that promote the peace and well-being and happiness, the knowledge, culture and industry, the dignity, value and station, of the entire human race. Thus, through the restoring waters of pure intention and unselfish effort, the earth of human potentialities will blossom with its own latent excellence and   8

---

4. Qur'án 41:53.
5. Qur'án 7:178; 8:22.

flower into praiseworthy qualities, and bear and flourish until it comes to rival that rosegarden of knowledge which belonged to our forefathers. Then will this holy land of Persia become in every sense the focal center of human perfections, reflecting as if in a mirror the full panoply of world civilization.

9   All praise and honor be to the Dayspring of divine wisdom, the Dawning Point of Revelation (Muḥammad), and to the holy line of His descendants, since, by the widespread rays of His consummate wisdom, His universal knowledge, those savage denizens of Yathrib (Medina) and Baṭhá (Mecca), miraculously, and in so brief a time, were drawn out of the depths of their ignorance, rose up to the pinnacles of learning, and became centers of arts and sciences and human perfections, and stars of felicity and true civilization, shining across the horizons of the world.

H is Majesty the Sháh[6] has, at the present 10 time, [1875] resolved to bring about the advancement of the Persian people, their welfare and security and the prosperity of their country. He has spontaneously extended assistance to his subjects, displaying energy and fair-mindedness, hoping that by the light of justice he might make Írán the envy of East and West, and set that fine fervor which characterized the first great epochs of Persia to flowing again through the veins of her people. As is clear to the discerning, the writer has for this reason felt it necessary to put down, for the sake of God alone and as a tribute to this high endeavor, a brief statement on certain urgent questions. To demonstrate that His one purpose is to promote the general welfare, He has withheld His name.[7] Since He believes that guidance toward righteousness is in itself a righteous act,

---

6. Náṣiri'd-Dín Sháh.

7. The original Persian text written in 1875 carried no author's name, and the first English translation published in 1910 under the title *The Mysterious Forces of Civilization* states only "Written in Persian by an Eminent Bahai Philosopher."

He offers these few words of counsel to His country's sons, words spoken for God's sake alone and in the spirit of a faithful friend. Our Lord, Who knows all things, bears witness that this Servant seeks nothing but what is right and good; for He, a wanderer in the desert of God's love, has come into a realm where the hand of denial or assent, of praise or blame, can touch Him not. "We nourish your souls for the sake of God; We seek from you neither recompense nor thanks."[8]

11   *"The hand is veiled, yet the pen writes as bidden;*
        The horse leaps forward, yet the rider's hidden."

12   O people of Persia! Look into those blossoming pages that tell of another day, a time long past. Read them and wonder; see the great sight. Írán in that day was as the heart of the world; she was the bright torch flaming in the assemblage of mankind. Her power and glory shone out like the morning above the world's horizons, and the splendor of her learning cast its rays over East and West.

---

8. Qur'án 76:9.

Word of the widespread empire of those who wore her crown reached even to the dwellers in the arctic circle, and the fame of the awesome presence of her King of Kings humbled the rulers of Greece and Rome. The greatest of the world's philosophers marveled at the wisdom of her government, and her political system became the model for all the kings of the four continents then known. She was distinguished among all peoples for the scope of her dominion, she was honored by all for her praiseworthy culture and civilization. She was as the pivot of the world, she was the source and center of sciences and arts, the wellspring of great inventions and discoveries, the rich mine of human virtues and perfections. The intellect, the wisdom of the individual members of this excellent nation dazzled the minds of other peoples, the brilliance and perceptive genius that characterized all this noble race aroused the envy of the whole world.

Aside from that which is a matter of record 13 in Persian histories, it is stated in the Old Testament—established today, among all European peoples, as a sacred and canonical Text—that in the time of Cyrus, called in Iranian works Bahman son of Isfandíyár, the three hundred and sixty divisions of the Persian Empire extended from the inner confines of India and China to the farthermost reaches of Yemen and Ethiopia.[9] The Greek accounts, as well, relate how this proud sovereign came against them with an innumerable host, and left their own till then victorious dominion level with the dust. He made the pillars of all the governments to quake; according to that authoritative Arab work, the history of Abu'l-Fidá, he took over the entire known world. It is likewise recorded in this same text and elsewhere, that Firaydún, a king of the Píshdádíyán Dynasty—who was indeed, for his inherent perfections, his powers of judgment, the scope of his knowledge, and his long series of continual victories, unique among all the rulers who preceded and followed him—divided the whole known world among his three sons.

14   As attested by the annals of the world's most illustrious peoples, the first government to be es-

---

9. 2 Chronicles 36:22–23; Ezra 1:2; Esther 1:1; 8:9; Isaiah 45:1, 14; 49:12.

tablished on earth, the foremost empire to be organized among the nations, was Persia's throne and diadem.

O people of Persia! Awake from your drunken 15 sleep! Rise up from your lethargy! Be fair in your judgment: will the dictates of honor permit this holy land, once the wellspring of world civilization, the source of glory and joy for all mankind, the envy of East and West, to remain an object of pity, deplored by all nations? She was once the noblest of peoples: will you let contemporary history register for the ages her now degenerate state? Will you complacently accept her present wretchedness, when she was once the land of all mankind's desire? Must she now, for this contemptible sloth, this failure to struggle, this utter ignorance, be accounted the most backward of nations?

Were not the people of Persia, in days long 16 gone, the head and front of intellect and wisdom? Did they not, by God's grace, shine out like the daystar from the horizons of divine knowledge? How is it that we are satisfied today with this miserable condition, are engrossed in our licentious passions, have blinded ourselves to supreme happiness, to that which is pleasing in God's sight, and have all become absorbed in our selfish concerns and the search for ignoble, personal advantage?

17 This fairest of lands was once a lamp, streaming with the rays of divine knowledge, of science and art, of nobility and high achievement, of wisdom and valor. Today, because of the idleness and lethargy of her people, their torpor, their undisciplined way of life, their lack of pride, lack of ambition—her bright fortune has been totally eclipsed, her light has turned to darkness. "The seven heavens and the seven earths weep over the mighty when he is brought low."

18 It should not be imagined that the people of Persia are inherently deficient in intelligence, or that for essential perceptiveness and understanding, inborn sagacity, intuition and wisdom, or innate capacity, they are inferior to others. God forbid! On the contrary, they have always excelled all other peoples in endowments conferred by birth. Persia herself, moreover, from the standpoint of her temperate climate and natural beauties, her geographical advantages and her rich soil, is blessed to a supreme degree. What she urgently requires, however, is deep reflection, resolute action, training, inspiration and encouragement.

Her people must make a massive effort, and their pride must be aroused.

Today throughout the five continents of the 19 globe it is Europe and most sections of America that are renowned for law and order, government and commerce, art and industry, science, philosophy and education. Yet in ancient times these were the most savage of the world's peoples, the most ignorant and brutish. They were even stigmatized as barbarians—that is, utterly rude and uncivilized. Further, from the fifth century after Christ until the fifteenth, that period defined as the Middle Ages, such terrible struggles and fierce upheavals, such ruthless encounters and horrifying acts, were the rule among the peoples of Europe, that the Europeans rightly describe those ten centuries as the Dark Ages. The basis of Europe's progress and civilization was actually laid in the fifteenth century of the Christian era, and from that time on, all her present evident culture has been, under the stimulus of great minds and as a result of the expansion of the frontiers of knowledge and the exertion of energetic and ambitious efforts, in the process of development.

Today by the grace of God and the spiritual 20 influence of His universal Manifestation, the fair-minded ruler of Írán has gathered his people into the shelter of justice, and the sincerity of the imperial purpose has shown itself in kingly acts. Hoping that his reign will rival the glorious past, he has sought to establish equity and righteousness and to foster education and the processes of civilization throughout this noble land, and to translate from potentiality into actuality whatever will insure its progress. Not until now had we seen a monarch, holding in his capable hands the reins of affairs, and on whose high resolve the welfare of all his subjects depends, exerting as it would befit him, like a benevolent father, his efforts toward the training and cultivation of his people, seeking to insure their well-being and peace of mind, and exhibiting due concern for their interests; this Servant and those like Him have therefore remained silent. Now, however, it is clear to the discerning that the Sháh has of his own accord determined to establish a just government and to secure the progress of all his subjects. His honorable intention has consequently evoked this present statement.

21   It is indeed strange that instead of offering thanks for this bounty, which truly derives from the grace of Almighty God, by arising as one in

gratitude and enthusiasm and praying that these noble purposes will daily multiply, some, on the contrary, whose reason has been corrupted by personal motives and the clarity of whose perception has been clouded by self-interest and conceit; whose energies are devoted to the service of their passions, whose sense of pride is perverted to the love of leadership, have raised the standard of opposition and waxed loud in their complaints. Up to now, they blamed the S͟háh for not, on his own initiative, working for his people's welfare and seeking to bring about their peace and well-being. Now that he has inaugurated this great design they have changed their tune. Some say that these are newfangled methods and foreign isms, quite unrelated to the present needs and the time-honored customs of Persia. Others have rallied the helpless masses, who know nothing of religion or its laws and basic principles and therefore have no power of discrimination—and tell them that these modern methods are the practices of heathen peoples, and are contrary to the venerated canons of true faith, and they add the saying, "He who imitates a people is one of them." One group insists that such reforms should go forward with great deliberation, step by step, haste being inadmissible. Another maintains that only such measures should be adopted as the Persians themselves devise, that they themselves should reform their political administration and their educational system and the state of their culture and that there is no need to borrow improvements from other nations. Every faction, in short, follows its own particular illusion.

22   O people of Persia! How long will you wander? How long must your confusion last? How long will it go on, this conflict of opinions, this useless antagonism, this ignorance, this refusal to think? Others are alert, and we sleep our dreamless sleep. Other nations are making every effort to improve their condition; we are trapped in our desires and self-indulgences, and at every step we stumble into a new snare.

23   God is Our witness that We have no ulterior motive in developing this theme. We seek neither to curry favor with any one nor to attract any one to Ourselves nor to derive any material benefit therefrom. We speak only as one earnestly desiring the good pleasure of God, for We have turned Our gaze away from the world and its peoples and have sought refuge in the sheltering care of

the Lord. "No pay do I ask of you for This . . . My reward is of God alone."[10]

Those who maintain that these modern concepts apply only to other countries and are irrelevant in Írán, that they do not satisfy her requirements or suit her way of life, disregard the fact that other nations were once as we are now. Did not these new systems and procedures, these progressive enterprises, contribute to the advancement of those countries? Were the people of Europe harmed by the adoption of such measures? Or did they rather by these means reach the highest degree of material development? Is it not true that for centuries, the people of Persia have lived as we see them living today, carrying out the pattern of the past? Have any discernible benefits resulted, has any progress been made? If these things had not been tested by experience, some in whose minds the light of native intelligence is clouded, might idly question them. On the contrary, however, every aspect of these prerequisites

24

10. Qur'án 6:90; 11:31.

to progress have in other countries been time and
again put to the test, and their benefits demonstrated so plainly that even the dullest mind can
grasp them.

25   Let us consider this justly and without bias: let
us ask ourselves which one of these basic principles and sound, well-established procedures
would fail to satisfy our present needs, or would
be incompatible with Persia's best political interests or injurious to the general welfare of her
people. Would the extension of education, the
development of useful arts and sciences, the promotion of industry and technology, be harmful
things? For such endeavor lifts the individual
within the mass and raises him out of the depths
of ignorance to the highest reaches of knowledge
and human excellence. Would the setting up of
just legislation, in accord with the divine laws
which guarantee the happiness of society and protect the rights of all mankind and are an impregnable proof against assault—would such laws,
insuring the integrity of the members of society
and their equality before the law, inhibit their
prosperity and success?

26   Or if by using one's perceptive faculties, one
can draw analogies from present circumstances

and the conclusions arrived at by collective experience, and can envisage as coming realities situations now only potential, would it be unreasonable to take such present measures as would guarantee our future security? Would it seem shortsighted, improvident and unsound, would it constitute a deviation from what is right and proper, if we were to strengthen our relationships with neighboring countries, enter into binding treaties with the great powers, foster friendly connections with well-disposed governments, look to the expansion of trade with the nations of East and West, develop our natural resources and increase the wealth of our people?

Would it spell perdition for our subjects if the provincial and district governors were relieved of their present absolute authority, whereby they function exactly as they please, and were instead limited to equity and truth, and if their sentences involving capital punishment, imprisonment and the like were contingent on confirmation by the Sháh and by higher courts in the capital, who would first duly investigate the case and determine the nature and seriousness of the crime, and then hand down a just decision subject to the issuance of a decree by the sovereign? If bribery and corruption, known today by the pleasant names of gifts and favors, were forever excluded, would this threaten the foundations of justice? Would it be an evidence of unsound thinking to deliver the soldiery, who are a living sacrifice to the state and the people and brave death at every turn, from their present extreme misery and indigence, and to make adequate arrangements for their sustenance, clothing and housing, and exert every effort to instruct their officers in military science, and supply them with the most advanced types of firearms and other weapons?

28   Should anyone object that the above-mentioned reforms have never yet been fully effected, he should consider the matter impartially and know that these deficiencies have resulted from the total absence of a unified public opinion, and the lack of zeal and resolve and devotion in the country's leaders. It is obvious that not until the people are educated, not until public opinion is rightly focused, not until government officials, even minor ones, are free from even the least remnant of corruption, can the country be properly administered. Not until discipline, order and good government reach the degree where an individual, even if he should put forth his utmost efforts to

do so, would still find himself unable to deviate by so much as a hair's breadth from righteousness, can the desired reforms be regarded as fully established.

Furthermore, any agency whatever, though it be the instrument of mankind's greatest good, is capable of misuse. Its proper use or abuse depends on the varying degrees of enlightenment, capacity, faith, honesty, devotion and high-mindedness of the leaders of public opinion. 29

The Sháh has certainly done his part, and the execution of the proposed beneficial measures is now in the hands of persons functioning in assemblies of consultation. If these individuals prove to be pure and high-minded, if they remain free from the taint of corruption, the confirmations of God will make them a never-failing source of bounty to mankind. He will cause to issue from their lips and their pens what will bless the people, so that every corner of this noble country of Írán will be illumined with their justice and integrity and the rays of that light will encompass the whole earth. "Neither will this be difficult with God."[11] 30

---

11. Qur'án 14:23; 35:18.

31   Otherwise it is clear that the results will prove unacceptable. For it has been directly witnessed in certain foreign countries that following on the establishment of parliaments those bodies actually distressed and confused the people and their well-meant reforms produced maleficent results. While the setting up of parliaments, the organizing of assemblies of consultation, constitutes the very foundation and bedrock of government, there are several essential requirements which these institutions must fulfill. First, the elected members must be righteous, God-fearing, high-minded, incorruptible. Second, they must be fully cognizant, in every particular, of the laws of God, informed as to the highest principles of law, versed in the rules which govern the management of internal affairs and the conduct of foreign relations, skilled in the useful arts of civilization, and content with their lawful emoluments.

32   Let it not be imagined that members of this type would be impossible to find. Through the grace of God and His chosen ones, and the high endeavors of the devoted and the consecrated, every difficulty can be easily resolved, every problem however complex will prove simpler than blinking an eye.

If, however, the members of these consulta- 33
tive assemblies are inferior, ignorant, uninformed
of the laws of government and administration,
unwise, of low aim, indifferent, idle, self-seek-
ing, no benefit will accrue from the organizing of
such bodies. Where, in the past, if a poor man
wanted his rights he had only to offer a gift to
one individual, now he would either have to re-
nounce all hope of justice or else satisfy the entire
membership.

Close investigation will show that the primary 34
cause of oppression and injustice, of unrighteous-
ness, irregularity and disorder, is the people's
lack of religious faith and the fact that they are
uneducated. When, for example, the people are
genuinely religious and are literate and well-
schooled, and a difficulty presents itself, they can
apply to the local authorities; if they do not meet
with justice and secure their rights and if they see
that the conduct of the local government is incompatible with the divine good pleasure and the
king's justice, they can then take their case to
higher courts and describe the deviation of the
local administration from the spiritual law.
Those courts can then send for the local records
of the case and in this way justice will be done.

25

At present, however, because of their inadequate schooling, most of the population lack even the vocabulary to explain what they want.

35   As to those persons who, here and there, are considered leaders of the people: because this is only the beginning of the new administrative process, they are not yet sufficiently advanced in their education to have experienced the delights of dispensing justice or to have tasted the exhilaration of promoting righteousness or to have drunk from the springs of a clear conscience and a sincere intent. They have not properly understood that man's supreme honor and real happiness lie in self-respect, in high resolves and noble purposes, in integrity and moral quality, in immaculacy of mind. They have, rather, imagined that their greatness consists in the accumulation, by whatever means may offer, of worldly goods.

36   A man should pause and reflect and be just: his Lord, out of measureless grace, has made him a human being and honored him with the words: "Verily, We created man in the goodliest of forms"[12] —and caused His mercy which rises out

---

12. Qur'án 95:4.

of the dawn of oneness to shine down upon him, until he became the wellspring of the words of God and the place where the mysteries of heaven alighted, and on the morning of creation he was covered with the rays of the qualities of perfection and the graces of holiness. How can he stain this immaculate garment with the filth of selfish desires, or exchange this everlasting honor for infamy? "Dost thou think thyself only a puny form, when the universe is folded up within thee?"[13]

Were it not our purpose to be brief and to de- 37 velop our primary subject, we would here set down a summary of themes from the divine world, as to the reality of man and his high station and the surpassing value and worth of the human race. Let this be, for another time.

The highest station, the supreme sphere, the 38 noblest, most sublime position in creation, whether visible or invisible, whether alpha or omega, is that of the Prophets of God, notwithstanding the fact that for the most part they have to outward seeming been possessed of nothing but their own poverty. In the same way, ineffable

---

13. The Imám 'Alí.

27

glory is set apart for the Holy Ones and those who are nearest to the Threshold of God, although such as these have never for a moment concerned themselves with material gain. Then comes the station of those just kings whose fame as protectors of the people and dispensers of divine justice has filled the world, whose name as powerful champions of the people's rights has echoed through creation. These give no thought to amassing enormous fortunes for themselves; they believe, rather, that their own wealth lies in enriching their subjects. To them, if every individual citizen has affluence and ease, the royal coffers are full. They take no pride in gold and silver, but rather in their enlightenment and their determination to achieve the universal good.

39   Next in rank are those eminent and honorable ministers of state and representatives, who place the will of God above their own, and whose administrative skill and wisdom in the conduct of their office raises the science of government to new heights of perfection. They shine in the learned world like lamps of knowledge; their thinking, their attitudes and their acts demonstrate their patriotism and their concern for the country's advancement. Content with a modest

stipend, they consecrate their days and nights to the execution of important duties and the devising of methods to insure the progress of the people. Through the effectiveness of their wise counsel, the soundness of their judgment, they have ever caused their government to become an example to be followed by all the governments of the world. They have made their capital city a focal center of great world undertakings, they have won distinction, attaining a supreme degree of personal eminence, and reaching the loftiest heights of repute and character.

Again, there are those famed and accomplished 40 men of learning, possessed of praiseworthy qualities and vast erudition, who lay hold on the strong handle of the fear of God and keep to the ways of salvation. In the mirror of their minds the forms of transcendent realities are reflected, and the lamp of their inner vision derives its light from the sun of universal knowledge. They are busy by night and by day with meticulous research into such sciences as are profitable to mankind, and they devote themselves to the training of students of capacity. It is certain that to their discerning taste, the proffered treasures of kings would not compare with a single drop of the waters of knowledge, and mountains of gold and silver could not outweigh the successful solution of a difficult problem. To them, the delights that lie outside their work are only toys for children, and the cumbersome load of unnecessary possessions is only good for the ignorant and base. Content, like the birds, they give thanks for a handful of seeds, and the song of their wisdom dazzles the minds of the world's most wise.

41   Again, there are sagacious leaders among the people and influential personalities throughout the country, who constitute the pillars of state. Their rank and station and success depend on their being the well-wishers of the people and in their seeking out such means as will improve the nation and will increase the wealth and comfort of the citizens.

42   Observe the case when an individual is an eminent person in his country, zealous, wise, pure-hearted, known for his innate capacity, intelligence, natural perspicacity—and is also an important member of the state: what, for such an individual, can be regarded as honor, abiding happiness, rank and station, whether in the here or the hereafter? Is it a diligent attention to truth and righteousness, is it dedication and resolve and

devotion to the good pleasure of God, is it the desire to attract the favorable consideration of the ruler and to merit the approval of the people? Or would it, rather, consist in this, that for the sake of indulging in feasts and dissipations by night he should undermine his country and break the hearts of his people by day, causing his God to reject him, and his sovereign to cast him out and his people to defame him and hold him in deserved contempt? By God, the moldering bones in the graveyard are better than such as these! Of what value are they, who have never tasted the heavenly food of truly human qualities, and never drunk of the crystalline waters of those bounties which belong to the realm of man?

It is unquestionable that the object in establishing parliaments is to bring about justice and righteousness, but everything hinges on the efforts of the elected representatives. If their intention is sincere, desirable results and 43 unforeseen improvements will be forthcoming; if not, it is certain that the whole thing will be meaningless, the country will come to a standstill and public affairs will continuously deteriorate. "I see a thousand builders unequal to one subverter; what then of the one builder who is followed by a thousand subverters?"

44   The purpose of the foregoing statements is to demonstrate at least this, that the happiness and greatness, the rank and station, the pleasure and peace, of an individual have never consisted in his personal wealth, but rather in his excellent character, his high resolve, the breadth of his learning, and his ability to solve difficult problems. How well has it been said: "On my back is a garment which, were it sold for a penny, that penny would be worth far more; yet within the garment is a soul which, if you weighed it against all the souls in the world, would prove greater and nobler."

45   In the present writer's view it would be preferable if the election of nonpermanent members of consultative assemblies in sovereign states should be dependent on the will and choice of the people. For elected representatives will on this account be somewhat inclined to exercise justice,

lest their reputation suffer and they fall into disfavor with the public.

It should not be imagined that the writer's earlier remarks constitute a denunciation of wealth or a commendation of poverty. Wealth is praiseworthy in the highest degree, if it is acquired by an individual's own efforts and the grace of God, in commerce, agriculture, art and industry, and if it be expended for philanthropic purposes. Above all, if a judicious and resourceful individual should initiate measures which would universally enrich the masses of the people, there could be no undertaking greater than this, and it would rank in the sight of God as the supreme achievement, for such a benefactor would supply the needs and insure the comfort and well-being of a great multitude. Wealth is most commendable, provided the entire population is wealthy. If, however, a few have inordinate riches while the rest are impoverished, and no fruit or benefit accrues from that wealth, then it is only a liability to its possessor. If, on the other hand, it is expended for the promotion of knowledge, the founding of elementary and other schools, the encouragement of art and industry, the training of orphans and the poor—in brief, if it is dedicated to the

46

33

THE SECRET OF DIVINE CIVILIZATION

welfare of society—its possessor will stand out
before God and man as the most excellent of all
who live on earth and will be accounted as one of
the people of paradise.

47   As to those who maintain that the
        inauguration of reforms and the setting
        up of powerful institutions would in
reality be at variance with the good pleasure of
God and would contravene the laws of the divine
Law-Giver and run counter to basic religious
principles and to the ways of the Prophet—let
them consider how this could be the case. Would
such reforms contravene the religious law because
they would be acquired from foreigners and
would therefore cause us to be as they are, since
"He who imitates a people is one of them"? In
the first place these matters relate to the temporal
and material apparatus of civilization, the
implements of science, the adjuncts of progress
in the professions and the arts, and the orderly

conduct of government. They have nothing whatever to do with the problems of the spirit and the complex realities of religious doctrine. If it be objected that even where material affairs are concerned foreign importations are inadmissible, such an argument would only establish the ignorance and absurdity of its proponents. Have they forgotten the celebrated ḥadíth (Holy Tradition): "Seek after knowledge, even unto China"? It is certain that the people of China were, in the sight of God, among the most rejected of men, because they worshipped idols and were unmindful of the omniscient Lord. The Europeans are at least "Peoples of the Book," and believers in God and specifically referred to in the sacred verse, "Thou shalt certainly find those to be nearest in affection to the believers, who say, 'We are Christians.'"[14] It is therefore quite permissible and indeed more appropriate to acquire knowledge from Christian countries. How could seeking after knowledge among the heathen be acceptable to God, and seeking it

---

14. Qur'án 5:85.

among the People of the Book be repugnant to Him?

48   Furthermore, in the Battle of the Confederates, Abú Sufyán enlisted the aid of the Baní Kinánih, the Baní Qahtán and the Jewish Baní Qurayzih and rose up with all the tribes of the Quraysh to put out the divine Light that flamed in the lamp of Yathrib (Medina). In those days the great winds of trials and tribulations were blowing from every direction, as it is written: "Do men think when they say 'We believe' they shall be let alone and not be put to proof?"[15] The believers were few and the enemy attacking in force, seeking to blot out the new-risen Sun of Truth with the dust of oppression and tyranny. Then Salmán (the Persian) came into the presence of the Prophet—the Dawning-Point of revelation, the Focus of the endless splendors of grace—and he said that in Persia to protect themselves from an encroaching host they would dig a moat or trench about their lands, and that this had proved a highly efficient safeguard against surprise attacks. Did that Wellspring of universal wisdom, that

---

15. Qur'án 29:2.

Mine of divine knowledge say in reply that this was a custom current among idolatrous, fire-worshipping Magians and could therefore hardly be adopted by monotheists? Or did He rather immediately direct His followers to set about digging a trench? He even, in His Own blessed person, took hold of the tools and went to work beside them.

It is moreover a matter of record in the books of the various Islamic schools and the writings of leading divines and historians, that after the Light of the World had risen over Ḥijáz, flooding all mankind with Its brilliance, and creating through the revelation of a new divine law, new principles and institutions, a fundamental change throughout the world—holy laws were revealed which in some cases conformed to the practices of the Days of Ignorance.[16] Among these, Muḥammad respected the months of religious truce,[17] retained

---

16. Jáhilíyyih: the period of paganism in Arabia, prior to the advent of Muḥammad.

17. The pagan Arabs observed one separate and three consecutive months of truce, during which period pilgrimages were made to Mecca, and fairs, poetry contests and similar events took place.

the prohibition of swine's flesh, continued the use of the lunar calendar and the names of the months and so on. There is a considerable number of such laws specifically enumerated in the texts:

50   "The people of the Days of Ignorance engaged in many practices which the law of Islám later confirmed. They would not take in marriage both a mother and her daughter, and the most shameful of acts in their view was to marry two sisters. They would stigmatize a man marrying the wife of his father, derisively calling him his father's competitor. It was their custom to go on pilgrimage to the House at Mecca, where they would perform the ceremonies of visitation, putting on the pilgrim's dress, practicing the circumambulation, running between the hills, pausing at all the stopping-places, and casting the stones. It was, furthermore, their wont to intercalate one month in every three-year period, to perform ablutions after intercourse, to rinse out the mouth and snuff up water through the nostrils, to part the hair, use the tooth-stick, pare the nails and pluck the armpits. They would, likewise, cut off the right hand of a thief."

51   Can one, God forbid, assume that because some of the divine laws resemble the practices of

the Days of Ignorance, the customs of a people abhorred by all nations, it follows that there is a defect in these laws? Or can one, God forbid, imagine that the Omnipotent Lord was moved to comply with the opinions of the heathen? The divine wisdom takes many forms. Would it have been impossible for Muḥammad to reveal a law which bore no resemblance whatever to any practice current in the Days of Ignorance? Rather, the purpose of His consummate wisdom was to free the people from the chains of fanaticism which had bound them hand and foot, and to forestall those very objections which today confuse the mind and trouble the conscience of the simple and helpless.

Some, who are not sufficiently informed as to the meaning of the divine Texts and the contents of traditional and written history, will aver that these customs of the Days of Ignorance were laws which had come down from His Holiness Abraham and had been retained by the idolaters. In this connection they will cite the Qur'ánic verse: "Follow the religion of Abraham, the sound in faith."[18] Nevertheless it is a fact attested by the

---

18. Qur'án 16:124.

writings of all the Islamic schools that the months of truce, the lunar calendar, and the cutting off of the right hand as punishment for theft, formed no part of Abraham's law. In any case, the Pentateuch is extant and available today, and contains the laws of Abraham. Let them refer to it. They will then, of course, insist that the Torah has been tampered with, and in proof will quote the Qur'ánic verse: "They pervert the text of the Word of God."[19] It is, however, known where such distortion has occurred, and is a matter of record in critical texts and commentaries.[20] Were We to develop the subject beyond this brief reference, We would have to abandon Our present purpose.

53   According to some accounts, mankind has been directed to borrow various good qualities and ways from wild animals, and to learn a lesson from these. Since it is permissible to imitate virtues of dumb animals, it is certainly far more so to borrow material sciences and techniques from foreign peoples, who at least belong to the human race and are distinguished by judgment and the

---

19. Qur'án 4:45; 5:16.
20. Cf. Bahá'u'lláh, *The Kitáb-i-Íqán*, p. 86.

power of speech. And if it be contended that such praiseworthy qualities are inborn in animals, by what proof can they claim that these essential principles of civilization, this knowledge and these sciences current among other peoples, are not inborn? Is there any Creator save God? Say: Praised be God!

The most learned and accomplished divines, the most distinguished scholars, have diligently studied those branches of knowledge the root and origin of which were the Greek philosophers such as Aristotle and the rest, and have regarded the acquisition from the Greek texts of sciences such as medicine, and branches of mathematics including algebra[21] and arithmetic, as a most valuable 54

---

21. "If by the word *algebra* we mean that branch of mathematics by which we learn how to solve the equation $x^2+5x=14$, written in this way, the science begins in the 17th century. If we allow the equation to be written with other and less convenient symbols, it may be considered as beginning at least as early as the 3rd century. If we permit it to be stated in words and solved, for simple cases of positive roots, by the aid of geometric figures, the science was known to Euclid and others of the Alexandrian school as early as 300 B.C. If we permit of more or less scientific guessing in achieving a solution, algebra may be said to have been known nearly

achievement. Every one of the eminent divines both studies and teaches the science of logic, although they consider its founder to have been a Sabean. Most of them have insisted that if a scholar has thoroughly mastered a variety of sciences but is not well grounded in logic, his opinions, deductions and conclusions cannot safely be relied upon.

55 It has now been clearly and irrefutably shown that the importation from foreign countries of the principles and procedures of civil-

---

2000 years B.C., and it had probably attracted the attention of the intellectual class much earlier . . . The name 'algebra' is quite fortuitous. When Mohammed ibn Mûsâ al-Khowârizmî . . . wrote in Baghdad (c. 825) he gave to one of his works the name *Al-jebr w'al-muqâbalah*. The title is sometimes translated as 'restoration and equation,' but the meaning was not clear even to the later Arab writers." Encyclopedia Britannica, 1952, s.v. Algebra.

ization, and the acquisition from them of sciences and techniques—in brief, of whatsoever will contribute to the general good—is entirely permissible. This has been done to focus public attention on a matter of such universal advantage, so that the people may arise with all their energies to further it, until, God helping them, this Sacred Land may within a brief period become the first of nations.

O you who are wise! Consider this carefully: 56 can an ordinary gun compare with a Martini-Henry rifle or a Krupp gun? If anyone should maintain that our old-time firearms are good enough for us and that it is useless to import weapons which have been invented abroad would even a child listen to him? Or should anyone say: "We have always transported merchandise from one country to another on the backs of animals. Why do we need steam engines? Why should we try to ape other peoples?" could any intelligent person tolerate such a statement? No, by the one God! Unless he should, because of some hidden design or animosity, refuse to accept the obvious.

Foreign nations, in spite of their having achieved 57 the greatest expertness in science, industry and the arts, do not hesitate to borrow ideas from one another. How can Persia, a country in the direst need, be allowed to lag behind, neglected, abandoned?

58   Those eminent divines and men of learning who walk the straight pathway and are versed in the secrets of divine wisdom and informed of the inner realities of the sacred Books; who wear in their hearts the jewel of the fear of God, and whose luminous faces shine with the lights of salvation—these are alert to the present need and they understand the requirements of modern times, and certainly devote all their energies toward encouraging the advancement of learning and civilization. "Are they equal, those who know, and those who do not know? . . . Or is the darkness equal with the light?"[22]

59   The spiritually learned are lamps of guidance among the nations, and stars of good fortune shining from the horizons of humankind. They are fountains of life for such as lie in the death of ignorance and unawareness, and clear springs of perfections for those who thirst and wander in the wasteland of their defects and errors. They

---

22. Qur'án 39:12; 13:17.

are the dawning places of the emblems of divine Unity and initiates in the mysteries of the glorious Qur'án. They are skilled physicians for the ailing body of the world, they are the sure antidote to the poison that has corrupted human society. It is they who are the strong citadel guarding humanity, and the impregnable sanctuary for the sorely distressed, the anxious and tormented, victims of ignorance. "Knowledge is a light which God casteth into the heart of whomsoever He willeth."

For every thing, however, God has created a 60 sign and symbol, and established standards and tests by which it may be known. The spiritually learned must be characterized by both inward and outward perfections; they must possess a good character, an enlightened nature, a pure intent, as well as intellectual power, brilliance and discernment, intuition, discretion and foresight, temperance, reverence, and a heartfelt fear of God. For an unlit candle, however great in diameter and tall, is no better than a barren palm tree or a pile of dead wood.

> "The flower-faced may sulk or play the flirt, 61
> The cruel fair may bridle and coquet;

But coyness in the ugly is ill-met,
And pain in a blind eye's a double hurt." [23]

62   An authoritative Tradition states: "As for him who is one of the learned:[24] he must guard himself, defend his faith, oppose his passions and obey the commandments of his Lord. It is then the duty of the people to pattern themselves after him." Since these illustrious and holy words embody all the conditions of learning, a brief commentary on their meaning is appropriate. Whoever is lacking in these divine qualifications and does not demonstrate these inescapable requirements in his own life, should not be referred to as learned and is not worthy to serve as a model for the believers.

63   The first of these requirements is to guard one's own self. It is obvious that this does not refer to protecting oneself from calamities and material tests, for the Prophets and saints were, each and every one, subjected to the bitterest afflictions that the world has to offer, and were targets for all the

---

23. Rúmí, The *Mathnaví*, I, 1906–1907.

24. 'Ulamá, from the Arabic, may be translated as "learned men," "scientists," or "religious authorities."

cruelties and aggressions of mankind. They sacrificed their lives for the welfare of the people, and with all their hearts they hastened to the place of their martyrdom; and with their inward and outward perfections they arrayed humanity in new garments of excellent qualities, both acquired and inborn. The primary meaning of this guarding of oneself is to acquire the attributes of spiritual and material perfection.

The first attribute of perfection is learning and 64 the cultural attainments of the mind, and this eminent station is achieved when the individual combines in himself a thorough knowledge of those complex and transcendental realities pertaining to God, of the fundamental truths of Qur'ánic political and religious law, of the contents of the sacred Scriptures of other faiths, and of those regulations and procedures which would contribute to the progress and civilization of this distinguished country. He should in addition be informed as to the laws and principles, the customs, conditions and manners, and the material and moral virtues characterizing the statecraft of other nations, and should be well versed in all the useful branches of learning of the day, and study the historical records of bygone governments and peoples. For if a learned individual has no knowledge of the sacred Scriptures and the entire field of divine and natural science, of religious jurisprudence and the arts of government and the varied learning of the time and the great events of history, he might prove unequal to an emergency, and this is inconsistent with the necessary qualification of comprehensive knowledge.

65 If for example a spiritually learned Muslim is conducting a debate with a Christian and he knows nothing of the glorious melodies of the Gospel, he will, no matter how much he imparts of the Qur'án and its truths, be unable to convince the Christian, and his words will fall on deaf ears. Should, however, the Christian observe that the Muslim is better versed in the fundamentals of Christianity than the Christian priests themselves, and understands the purport of the Scriptures even better than they, he will gladly accept the Muslim's arguments, and he would indeed have no other recourse.

66 When the Chief of the Exile[25] came into the presence of that Luminary of divine wisdom, of

_____

25. The Resh Galuta, a prince or ruler of the exiles in Babylon, to whom Jews, wherever they were, paid tribute.

salvation and certitude, the Imám Riḍá—had the Imám, that mine of knowledge, failed in the course of their interview to base his arguments on authority appropriate and familiar to the Exilarch, the latter would never have acknowledged the greatness of His Holiness.

The state is, moreover, based upon two potent forces, the legislative and the executive. The focal center of the executive power is the government, while that of the legislative is the learned—and if this latter great support and pillar should prove defective, how is it conceivable that the state should stand? 67

In view of the fact that at the present time such fully developed and comprehensively learned individuals are hard to come by, and the government and people are in dire need of order and direction, it is essential to establish a body of scholars the various groups of whose membership 68 would each be expert in one of the aforementioned branches of knowledge. This body should with the greatest energy and vigor deliberate as to all present and future requirements, and bring about equilibrium and order.

69   Up to now the religious law has not been given a decisive role in our courts, because each of the ulama has been handing down decrees as he saw fit, based on his arbitrary interpretation and personal opinion. For example, two men will go to law, and one of the ulama will find for the plaintiff and another for the defendant. It may even happen that in one and the same case two conflicting decisions will be handed down by the same mujtahid, on the grounds that he was inspired first in one direction and then in the other. There can be no doubt that this state of affairs has confused every important issue and must jeopardize the very foundations of society. For neither the plaintiff nor the defendant ever loses hope of eventual success, and each in turn will waste his life in the attempt to secure a later verdict which would reverse the previous one. Their entire time is thus given over to litigation, with the result that their life instead of being devoted to beneficial undertakings and necessary personal affairs, is com-

pletely involved with the dispute. Indeed, these two litigants might just as well be dead, for they can serve their government and community not a particle. If, however, a definite and final verdict were forthcoming, the duly convicted party would perforce give up all hope of reopening the case, and would then be relieved on that score and would go back to looking after his own concerns and those of others.

Since the primary means for securing the peace 70 and tranquillity of the people, and the most effective agency for the advancement of high and low alike, is this all-important matter, it is incumbent on those learned members of the great consultative assembly who are thoroughly versed in the divine law to evolve a single, direct and definite procedure for the settlement of litigations. This instrument should then be published throughout the country by order of the king, and its provisions should be strictly adhered to. This all-important question requires the most urgent attention.

The second attribute of perfection is justice 71 and impartiality. This means to have no regard for one's own personal benefits and selfish advantages, and to carry out the laws of God without the slightest concern for anything else. It means to see one's self as only one of the servants of God, the All-Possessing, and except for aspiring to spiritual distinction, never attempting to be singled out from the others. It means to consider the welfare of the community as one's own. It means, in brief, to regard humanity as a single individual, and one's own self as a member of that corporeal form, and to know of a certainty that if pain or injury afflicts any member of that body, it must inevitably result in suffering for all the rest.

72   The third requirement of perfection is to arise with complete sincerity and purity of purpose to educate the masses: to exert the utmost effort to instruct them in the various branches of learning and useful sciences, to encourage the development of modern progress, to widen the scope of commerce, industry and the arts, to further such measures as will increase the people's wealth. For the mass of the population is uninformed as to these vital agencies which would constitute an immediate remedy for society's chronic ills.

73   It is essential that scholars and the spiritually learned should undertake in all sincerity and pu-

rity of intent and for the sake of God alone, to counsel and exhort the masses and clarify their vision with that collyrium which is knowledge. For today the people out of the depths of their superstition, imagine that any individual who believes in God and His signs, and in the Prophets and divine Revelations and laws, and is a devout and God-fearing person, must of necessity remain idle and spend his days in sloth, so as to be considered in the sight of God as one who has forsaken the world and its vanities, set his heart on the life to come, and isolated himself from human beings in order to draw nearer to God. Since this theme will be developed elsewhere in the present text, We shall leave it for the moment.

Other attributes of perfection are to fear God, 74 to love God by loving His servants, to exercise mildness and forbearance and calm, to be sincere, amenable, clement and compassionate; to have resolution and courage, trustworthiness and energy, to strive and struggle, to be generous, loyal, without malice, to have zeal and a sense of honor, to be high-minded and magnanimous, and to have regard for the rights of others. Whoever is lacking in these excellent human qualities is defective. If We were to explain the inner meanings of each one of these attributes, "the poem would take up seventy maunds[26] of paper."

75   The second of these spiritual standards which apply to the possessor of knowledge is that he should be the defender of his faith. It is obvious that these holy words do not refer exclusively to searching out the implications of the law, observing the forms of worship, avoiding greater and lesser sins, practicing the religious ordinances, and by all these methods, protecting the Faith. They mean rather that the whole population should be protected in every way; that every effort should be exerted to adopt a combination of all possible measures to raise up the Word of God, increase

---

26. A measure of weight, in Ṭihrán equivalent to six and two-thirds pounds.

the number of believers, promote the Faith of God and exalt it and make it victorious over other religions.

If, indeed, the Muslim religious authorities had 76 persevered along these lines as they ought to have done, by now every nation on earth would have been gathered into the shelter of the unity of God and the bright fire of "that He may make it victorious over every other religion"[27] would have flamed out like the sun in the midmost heart of the world.

Fifteen centuries after Christ, Luther, who was 77 originally one of the twelve members of a Catholic religious body at the center of the Papal government and later on initiated the Protestant religious belief, opposed the Pope on certain points of doctrine such as the prohibition of monastic marriage, the revering and bowing down before images of the Apostles and Christian leaders of the past, and various other religious practices and ceremonies which were accretional to the ordinances of the Gospel. Although at that period the power of the Pope was so great and he was

---

27. Qur'án 9:33; 48:28; 61:9.

regarded with such awe that the kings of Europe shook and trembled before him, and he held control of all Europe's major concerns in the grasp of his might—nevertheless because Luther's position as regards the freedom of religious leaders to marry, the abstention from worshipping and making prostrations before images and representations hung in the churches, and the abrogation of ceremonials which had been added on to the Gospel, was demonstrably correct, and because the proper means were adopted for the promulgation of his views: within these last four hundred and some years the majority of the population of America, four-fifths of Germany and England and a large percentage of Austrians, in sum about one hundred and twenty-five million people drawn from other Christian denominations, have entered the Protestant Church. The leaders of this religion are still making every effort to promote it, and today on the East Coast of Africa, ostensibly to emancipate the Sudanese and various Negro peoples, they have established schools and colleges and are training and civilizing completely savage African tribes, while their true and primary purpose is to convert some of the Muslim Negro tribes to Protestantism. Every community is toiling for the advancement of its people, and we (i.e., Muslims) sleep on!

Although it was not clear what purpose impelled this man or where he was tending, see how the zealous efforts of Protestant leaders have spread his doctrines far and wide. 78

Now if the illustrious people of the one true God, the recipients of His confirmations, the objects of His divine assistance, should put forth all their strength, and with complete dedication, relying upon God and turning aside from all else but Him, should adopt procedures for spreading the Faith and should bend all their efforts to this end, it is certain that His divine light would envelop the whole earth. 79

A few, who are unaware of the reality below the surface of events, who cannot feel the pulse of the world under their fingers, who do not know what a massive dose of truth must be administered to heal this chronic old disease of falsehood, believe that the Faith can only be spread by the sword, and bolster their opinion with the Tradition, "I am a Prophet by the sword." If, however, they would carefully examine this question, they would see that in this day and age the sword is not a suitable means for promulgating the Faith, 80

57

for it would only fill peoples' hearts with revulsion and terror. According to the divine law of Muḥammad, it is not permissible to compel the People of the Book to acknowledge and accept the Faith. While it is a sacred obligation devolving on every conscientious believer in the unity of God to guide mankind to the truth, the Traditions "I am a Prophet by the sword" and "I am commanded to threaten the lives of the people until they say, 'There is none other God but God'" referred to the idolaters of the Days of Ignorance, who in their blindness and bestiality had sunk below the level of human beings. A faith born of sword thrusts could hardly be relied upon, and would for any trifling cause revert to error and unbelief. After the ascension of Muḥammad, and His passing to "the seat of truth, in the presence of the potent King,"[28] the tribes around Medina apostatized from their Faith, turning back to the idolatry of pagan times.

81   Remember when the holy breaths of the Spirit of God (Jesus) were shedding their sweetness

---

28. Qur'án 54:55.

over Palestine and Galilee, over the shores of
Jordan and the regions around Jerusalem, and
the wondrous melodies of the Gospel were
sounding in the ears of the spiritually illumined,
all the peoples of Asia and Europe, of Africa
and America, of Oceania, which comprises the
islands and archipelagoes of the Pacific and
Indian Oceans, were fire-worshippers and pa-
gans, ignorant of the divine Voice that spoke
out on the Day of the Covenant.[29] Alone the
Jews believed in the divinity and oneness of
God. Following the declaration of Jesus, the pure
and reviving breath of His mouth conferred
eternal life on the inhabitants of those regions
for a period of three years, and through divine
Revelation the law of Christ, at that time the
vital remedy for the ailing body of the world,
was established. In the days of Jesus only a few
individuals turned their faces toward God; in
fact only the twelve disciples and a few women

---

29. Qur'án 7:171: Yawm-i-Alast, the Day when God,
addressing Adam's posterity-to-be, said to them, "Am I not
your Lord?" (a-lastu bi Rabbikum) and they replied: "Yea,
we bear witness."

truly became believers, and one of the disciples, Judas Iscariot apostatized from his Faith, leaving eleven. After the ascension of Jesus to the Realm of Glory, these few souls stood up with their spiritual qualities and with deeds that were pure and holy, and they arose by the power of God and the life-giving breaths of the Messiah to save all the peoples of the earth. Then all the idolatrous nations as well as the Jews rose up in their might to kill the divine fire that had been lit in the lamp of Jerusalem. "Fain would they put out God's light with their mouths: but God hath willed to perfect His light, albeit the infidels abhor it."[30] Under the fiercest tortures, they did every one of these holy souls to death; with butchers' cleavers, they chopped the pure and undefiled bodies of some of them to pieces and burned them in furnaces, and they stretched some of the followers on the rack and then buried them alive. In spite of this agonizing requital, the Christians continued to teach the Cause of God, and they never drew a sword from its scabbard or even so much as grazed a

---

30. Qur'án 9:33.

cheek. Then in the end the Faith of Christ encompassed the whole earth, so that in Europe and America no traces of other religions were left, and today in Asia and Africa and Oceania, large masses of people are living within the sanctuary of the Four Gospels.

It has now by the above irrefutable proofs 82 been fully established that the Faith of God must be propagated through human perfections, through qualities that are excellent and pleasing, and spiritual behavior. If a soul of his own accord advances toward God he will be accepted at the Threshold of Oneness, for such a one is free of personal considerations, of greed and selfish interests, and he has taken refuge within the sheltering protection of his Lord. He will become known among men as trustworthy and truthful, temperate and scrupulous, high-minded and loyal, incorruptible and God-fearing. In this way the primary purpose in revealing the divine law—which is to bring about happiness in the after life and civilization and the refinement of character in this—will be realized. As for the sword, it will only produce a man who is outwardly a believer, and inwardly a traitor and apostate.

83 We shall here relate a story that will serve as an example to all. The Arabian chronicles tell how, at a time prior to the advent of Muḥammad, Nuʻmán son of Mundhir the Lakhmite—an Arab king in the Days of Ignorance, whose seat of government was the city of Ḥírih—had one day returned so often to his wine-cup that his mind clouded over and his reason deserted him. In this drunken and insensible condition he gave orders that his two boon companions, his close and much-loved friends, Khálid son of Mudallil and ʻAmr son of Masʻúd-Kaldih, should be put to death. When he wakened after his carousal, he inquired for the two friends and was given the grievous news. He was sick at heart, and because of his intense love and longing for them, he built two splendid monuments over their two graves and he named these the Smeared-With-Blood.

84 Then he set apart two days out of the year, in memory of the two companions, and he called one of them the Day of Evil and one the Day of Grace. Every year on these two appointed days he would issue forth with pomp and circumstance and sit between the monuments. If, on the Day of Evil, his eye fell on any soul, that person would

be put to death; but on the Day of Grace, whoever passed would be overwhelmed with gifts and
benefits. Such was his rule, sealed with a mighty
oath and always rigidly observed.

One day the king mounted his horse, that was   85
called Maḥmúd, and rode out into the plains to
hunt. Suddenly in the distance he caught sight of
a wild donkey. Nuʿmán urged on his horse to over-
take it, and galloped away at such speed that he
was cut off from his retinue. As night approached,
the king was hopelessly lost. Then he made out a
tent, far off in the desert, and he turned his horse
and headed toward it. When he reached the en-
trance of the tent he asked, "Will you receive a
guest?" The owner (who was Ḥanzala, son of Abí-
Ghafráy-i-Ṭáʾí) replied, "Yea." He came forward
and helped Nuʿmán to dismount. Then he went
to his wife and told her, "There are clear signs of
greatness in the bearing of this person. Do your
best to show him hospitality, and make ready a
feast." His wife said, "We have a ewe. Sacrifice it.
And I have saved a little flour against such a day."
Ḥanzala first milked the ewe and carried a bowl
of milk to Nuʿmán, and then he slaughtered her
and prepared a meal; and what with his friendli-
ness and loving-kindness, Nuʿmán spent that

night in peace and comfort. When dawn came, Nu'mán made ready to leave, and he said to Ḥanzala: "You have shown me the utmost generosity, receiving and feasting me. I am Nu'mán, son of Mun<u>dh</u>ir, and I shall eagerly await your arrival at my court."

86   Time passed, and famine fell on the land of Ṭayy. Ḥanzala was in dire need and for this reason he sought out the king. By a strange coincidence he arrived on the Day of Evil. Nu'mán was greatly troubled in spirit. He began to reproach his friend, saying, "Why did you come to your friend on this day of all days? For this is the Day of Evil, that is, the Day of Wrath and the Day of Distress. This day, should my eyes alight on Qábús, my only son, he should not escape with his life. Now ask me whatever favor you will."

87   Ḥanzala said: "I knew nothing of your Day of Evil. As for the gifts of this life, they are meant for the living, and since I at this hour must drink of death, what can all the world's storehouses avail me now?"

88   Nu'mán said, "There is no help for this."

89   Ḥanzala told him: "Respite me, then, that I may go back to my wife and make my testament. Next year I shall return, on the Day of Evil."

Nu'mán then asked for a guarantor, so that, if 90
Ḥanzala should break his word, this guarantor
would be put to death instead. Ḥanzala, helpless
and bewildered, looked about him. Then his gaze
fell on one of Nu'mán's retinue, Sharík, son of
'Amr, son of Qays of Shaybán, and to him he
recited these lines: "O my partner, O son of 'Amr!
Is there any escape from death? O brother of
every afflicted one! O brother of him who is
brotherless! O brother of Nu'mán, in thee today
is a surety for the Shaykh. Where is Shaybán the
noble—may the All-Merciful favor him!" But
Sharík only answered, "O my brother, a man cannot gamble with his life." At this the victim could
not tell where to turn. Then a man named Qarád,
son of Adja' the Kalbite stood up and offered himself as a surety, agreeing that, should he fail on
the next Day of Wrath to deliver up the victim,
the king might do with him, Qarád, as he wished.
Nu'mán then bestowed five hundred camels on
Ḥanzala, and sent him home.

In the following year on the Day of Evil, as 91
soon as the true dawn broke in the sky, Nu'mán
as was his custom set out with pomp and pag-
eantry and made for the two mausoleums called
the Smeared-With-Blood. He brought Qarád

along, to wreak his kingly wrath upon him. The pillars of the state then loosed their tongues and begged for mercy, imploring the king to respite Qarád until sundown, for they hoped that Ḥan-zala might yet return; but the king's purpose was to spare the life of Ḥanzala, and to requite his hospitality by putting Qarád to death in his place. As the sun began to set, they stripped off the gar-ments of Qarád, and made ready to sever his head. At that moment a rider appeared in the distance, galloping at top speed. Nuʻmán said to the swords-man, "Why delayest thou?" The ministers said, "Perchance it is Ḥanzala who comes." And when the rider drew near, they saw it was none other.

92   Nuʻmán was sorely displeased. He said, "Thou fool! Thou didst slip away once from the clutch-ing fingers of death; must thou provoke him now a second time?"

93   And Ḥanzala answered, "Sweet in my mouth and pleasant on my tongue is the poison of death, at the thought of redeeming my pledge."

94   Nuʻmán asked, "What could be the reason for this trustworthiness, this regard for thine obliga-tion and this concern for thine oath?" And Ḥanzala answered, "It is my faith in the one God and in the Books that have come down from

66

heaven." Nu'mán asked, "What Faith dost thou profess?" And Ḥanzala said, "It was the holy breaths of Jesus that brought me to life. I follow the straight pathway of Christ, the Spirit of God." Nu'mán said, "Let me inhale these sweet aromas of the Spirit."

So it was that Ḥanzala drew out the white 95 hand of guidance from the bosom of the love of God,[31] and illumined the sight and the insight of the beholders with the Gospel light. After he had in bell-like accents recited some of the divine verses out of the Evangel, Nu'mán and all his ministers sickened of their idols and their idol-worship and were confirmed in the Faith of God. And they said, "Alas, a thousand

---

31. Cf. Qur'án 27:12, referring to Moses: "Put now thy hand into thy bosom: it shall come forth white . . . one of nine signs to Pharaoh and his people . . ." Also Qur'án 7:105; 20:23; 26:32; and 28:32. Also Exodus 4:6. See too Edward Fitzgerald's *The Rubaiyat of Omar Khayyam:* "Now the New Year reviving old Desires, / The thoughtful Soul to Solitude retires, / Where the White Hand of Moses on the Bough / Puts out, and Jesus from the Ground suspires." The metaphors here refer to white blossoms and the perfumes of spring.

times alas, that up to now we were careless of this infinite mercy and veiled away therefrom, and were bereft of this rain from the clouds of the grace of God." Then straightway the king tore down the two monuments called the Smeared-With-Blood, and he repented of his tyranny and established justice in the land.

96 Observe how one individual, and he a man of the desert, to outward seeming unknown and of no station—because he showed forth one of the qualities of the pure in heart, was able to deliver this proud sovereign and a great company of others from the dark night of unbelief and guide them into the morning of salvation; to save them from the perdition of idolatry and bring them to the shores of the oneness of God, and to put an end to practices of the sort which blight a whole society

and reduce the peoples to barbarism. One must think deeply over this, and grasp its meaning.

My heart aches, for I note with intense regret that the attention of the people is nowhere directed toward that which is worthy of this day and time. The Sun of Truth has risen above the world but we are ensnared in the dark of our imaginings. The waters of the Most Great Sea are surging all around us, while we are parched and weak with thirst. The divine bread is coming down from heaven, and yet we grope and stumble in a famine-stricken land. "Between the weeping and the telling, I spin out my days." 97

One of the principal reasons why people of other religions have shunned and failed to become converted to the Faith of God is fanaticism and unreasoning religious zeal. See for example the divine words that were addressed to Muḥammad, the Ark of Salvation, the Luminous Countenance 98 and Lord of Men, bidding Him to be gentle with the people and long-suffering: "Debate with them in the kindliest manner."[32] That Blessed Tree Whose light was "neither of the East nor of the West"[33] and Who cast over all the peoples of the earth the sheltering shade of a measureless grace, showed forth infinite kindness and forbearance in His dealings with every one. In these words, likewise, were Moses and Aaron commanded to challenge Pharaoh, Lord of the Stakes:[34] "Speak ye to him with gentle speech."[35]

99   Although the noble conduct of the Prophets and Holy Ones of God is widely known, and it is indeed, until the coming of the Hour,[36] in every

---

32. Qur'án 16:126.

33. Qur'án 24:35.

34. D͟hu'l-Awtád is variously rendered by translators of the Qur'án as The Impaler, The Contriver of the Stakes, The Lord of a Strong Dominion, The One Surrounded by Ministers, etc. Awtád means pegs or tent stakes. See Qur'án 38:11 and 89:9.

35. Qur'án 20:46.

36. Qur'án 33:63: "Men will ask Thee of 'the Hour.' Say: The knowledge of it is with God alone." Cf. also 22:1, "the earthquake of the Hour," etc. See also Matthew 24:36, 42, etc. To Bahá'ís, this refers to the Advent of the Báb and Bahá'u'lláh.

aspect of life an excellent pattern for all mankind to follow, nevertheless some have remained neglectful of and separated from these qualities of extraordinary sympathy and loving-kindness, and have been prevented from attaining to the inner significances of the Holy Books. Not only do they scrupulously shun the adherents of religions other than their own, they do not even permit themselves to show them common courtesy. If one is not allowed to associate with another, how can one guide him out of the dark and empty night of denial, of "there-is-no-God," into the bright morning of belief, and the affirmation, "but God."[37] And how can one urge him on and encourage him to rise up out of the abyss of perdition and ignorance and climb the heights of salvation and knowledge? Consider justly: had not Ḥanzala treated Nu'mán with true friendship, showing him kindness and hospitality, could he have brought the King and a great number of other idolaters to acknowledge the unity of God?

---

37. Cf. the Islamic confession of faith, sometimes called the two testimonies: "I testify that there is no God but God and Muḥammad is the Prophet of God."

To keep aloof from people, to shun them, to be harsh with them, will make them shrink away, while affection and consideration, mildness and forbearance will attract their hearts toward God. If a true believer when meeting an individual from a foreign country should express revulsion, and should speak the horrible words forbidding association with foreigners and referring to them as "unclean," the stranger would be grieved and offended to such a point that he would never accept the Faith, even if he should see, taking place before his very eyes, the miracle of the splitting of the moon. The results of shunning him would be this, that if there had been in his heart some faint inclination toward God, he would repent of it, and would flee away from the sea of faith into the wastes of oblivion and unbelief. And upon returning home to his own country he would publish in the press statements to the effect that such and such a nation was utterly lacking in the qualifications of a civilized people.

100　　If we ponder a while over the Qur'ánic verses and proofs, and the traditional accounts which have come down to us from those stars of the heaven of divine Unity, the Holy Imáms, we shall be convinced of the fact that if a soul is endowed with the attributes of true faith and characterized with spiritual qualities he will become to all mankind an emblem of the outstretched mercies of God. For the attributes of the people of faith are justice and fair-mindedness; forbearance and compassion and generosity; consideration for others; candor, trustworthiness, and loyalty; love and loving-kindness; devotion and determination and humanity. If therefore an individual is truly righteous, he will avail himself of all those means which will attract the hearts of men, and through the attributes of God he will draw them to the straight path of faith and cause them to drink from the river of everlasting life.

Today we have closed our eyes to every righteous act and have sacrificed the abiding happiness of society to our own transitory profit. We regard fanaticism and zealotry as redounding to our credit and honor, and not content with this, we denounce one another and plot each other's ruin, and whenever we wish to put on a show of wisdom and learning, of virtue and godliness, we set about mocking and reviling this one and that. "The ideas of such a one," we say, "are wide of the mark, and so-and-so's behavior leaves much to be desired. The religious observances of Zayd are few and far between, and 'Amr is not firm in his faith. So-and-so's opinions smack of Europe. Fundamentally, Blank thinks of nothing but his own name and fame. Last night when the congregation stood up to pray, the row was out of line, and it is not permissible to follow a different leader. No rich man has died this month, and nothing has been offered to charity in memory of the Prophet. The edifice of religion has crumbled, the foundations of faiths have been blown to the winds. The carpet of belief has been rolled up, the tokens of certitude blotted out; the whole world has fallen into error; when it comes to repelling tyranny all are soft and remiss. Days and months have passed away, and these villages and estates still belong to the same owners as they did last year. In this town there used to be seventy different governments functioning in good order, but the number has steadily decreased; there are only twenty-five left now, as a memento. It used to be that two hundred contradictory judgments were handed down by the same muftí in any one day, now we hardly get fifty. In those days there were crowds of people who were all brainsick with litigation, and now they rest in peace; today the plaintiff would be defeated and the defendant victorious, tomorrow the plaintiff won the case and the defendant lost it—but now this excellent practice has been abandoned too. What is this heathenish religion, this idolatrous kind of error! Alas for the law, alas for the Faith, alas for all these calamities! O Brothers in the Faith! This is surely the end of the world! The Judgment is coming!"

With words such as these they assault the minds 102 of the helpless masses and disturb the hearts of the already bewildered poor, who know nothing of the true state of affairs and the real basis for all such talk, and remain completely unaware of the fact that a thousand selfish purposes are concealed behind the supposedly religious eloquence of certain individuals. They imagine that speakers of this type are motivated by virtuous zeal, when the truth is that such individuals keep up a great hue and cry because they see their own personal ruin in the welfare of the masses, and believe that if the people's eyes are opened, their own light will go out. Only the keenest insight will detect the fact that if the hearts of these individuals were really impelled by righteousness and the fear of

God, the fragrance of it would, like musk, be spreading everywhere. Nothing in the world can ever be supported by words alone.

103   *But these ill-omened owls have done a wrong,*
    And learned to sing as the white falcon sings.
    And what of Sheba's message that the lapwing
      brings
    If the bittern learn to sing the lapwing's song?[38]

104   The spiritually learned, those who have derived infinite significance and wisdom from the Book of divine Revelation, and whose illumined hearts draw inspiration from the unseen world of God, certainly exert their efforts to bring about the supremacy of the true followers of God, in all respects and above all peoples, and they toil and struggle to make use of every agency that will conduce to progress. If any man neglects these high purposes he can never prove acceptable in the sight of God; he stands out with all his shortcomings and claims perfection, and destitute, pretends to wealth.

---

38. Cf. Qur'án 27:20 ff.

One sluggish, blind and surly's a poor thing, 105
"A lump of flesh, without a foot or wing."
How far is he who apes and makes a show
From the illumined, who doth truly know.
One but an echo, though it's clear and sharp,
And one, the Psalmist David with his harp.

Knowledge, purity, devotion, discipline, inde- 106
pendence, have nothing to do with outer appearance and dress. Once in the course of My travels
I heard an eminent personage make the following excellent remark, the wit and charm of which
remain in memory: "Not every cleric's turban is a
proof of continence and knowledge; not every
layman's hat a sign of ignorance and immorality.
How many a hat has proudly raised the banner
of knowledge, how many a turban pulled down
the law of God!"

The third element of the utterance under 107
discussion is, "opposes his passions."
How wonderful are the implications
of this deceptively easy, all-inclusive phrase. This
is the very foundation of every laudable human

quality; indeed, these few words embody the light of the world, the impregnable basis of all the spiritual attributes of human beings. This is the balance wheel of all behavior, the means of keeping all man's good qualities in equilibrium.

108 For desire is a flame that has reduced to ashes uncounted lifetime harvests of the learned, a devouring fire that even the vast sea of their accumulated knowledge could never quench. How often has it happened that an individual who was graced with every attribute of humanity and wore the jewel of true understanding, nevertheless followed after his passions until his excellent qualities passed beyond moderation and he was forced into excess. His pure intentions changed to evil ones, his attributes were no longer put to uses worthy of them, and the power of his desires turned him aside from righteousness and its rewards into ways that were dangerous and dark. A good character is in the sight of God and His chosen ones and the possessors of insight, the most excellent and praiseworthy of all things, but always on condition that its center of emanation should be reason and knowledge and its base should be true moderation. Were the implications of this subject to be developed as they deserve the

work would grow too long and our main theme would be lost to view.

All the peoples of Europe, notwithstanding 109 their vaunted civilization, sink and drown in this terrifying sea of passion and desire, and this is why all the phenomena of their culture come to nothing. Let no one wonder at this statement or deplore it. The primary purpose, the basic objective, in laying down powerful laws and setting up great principles and institutions dealing with every aspect of civilization, is human happiness; and human happiness consists only in drawing closer to the Threshold of Almighty God, and in securing the peace and well-being of every individual member, high and low alike, of the human race; and the supreme agencies for accomplishing these two objectives are the excellent qualities with which humanity has been endowed.

A superficial culture, unsupported by a culti- 110 vated morality, is as "a confused medley of dreams,"[39] and external luster without inner perfection is "like a vapor in the desert which the

_____

39. Qur'án 12:44; 21:5.

79

thirsty dreameth to be water."[40] For results which would win the good pleasure of God and secure the peace and well-being of man, could never be fully achieved in a merely external civilization.

111   The peoples of Europe have not advanced to the higher planes of moral civilization, as their opinions and behavior clearly demonstrate. Notice, for example, how the supreme desire of European governments and peoples today is to conquer and crush one another, and how, while harboring the greatest secret repulsion, they spend their time exchanging expressions of neighborly affection, friendship and harmony.

112   There is the well-known case of the ruler who is fostering peace and tranquillity and at the same time devoting more energy than the warmongers to the accumulation of weapons and the building up of a larger army, on the grounds that peace and harmony can only be brought about by force. Peace is the pretext, and night and day they are all straining every nerve to pile up more weapons of war, and to pay for this their wretched people must sacrifice most of whatever they are able to earn by their sweat and toil. How many thou-

---

40. Qur'án 24:39.

sands have given up their work in useful industries and are laboring day and night to produce new and deadlier weapons which would spill out the blood of the race more copiously than before.

Each day they invent a new bomb or explosive 113 and then the governments must abandon their obsolete arms and begin producing the new, since the old weapons cannot hold their own against the new. For example at this writing, in the year 1292 A.H.[41] they have invented a new rifle in Germany and a bronze cannon in Austria, which have greater firepower than the Martini-Henry rifle and the Krupp cannon, are more rapid in their effects and more efficient in annihilating humankind. The staggering cost of it all must be borne by the hapless masses.

Be just: can this nominal civilization, unsup- 114 ported by a genuine civilization of character, bring about the peace and well-being of the people or win the good pleasure of God? Does it not, rather, connote the destruction of man's estate and pull down the pillars of happiness and peace?

---

41. 1875 A.D.

115   At the time of the Franco-Prussian War, in the year 1870 of the Christian era, it was reported that 600,000 men died, broken and beaten, on the field of battle. How many a home was torn out by the roots; how many a city, flourishing the night before, was toppled down by sunrise. How many a child was orphaned and abandoned, how many an old father and mother had to see their sons, the young fruit of their lives, twisting and dying in dust and blood. How many women were widowed, left without a helper or protector.

116   And then there were the libraries and magnificent buildings of France that went up in flames, and the military hospital, packed with sick and wounded men, that was set on fire and burned to the ground. And there followed the terrible events of the Commune, the savage acts, the ruin and horror when opposing factions fought and killed one another in the streets of Paris. There were the hatreds and hostilities between Catholic religious leaders and the German government. There was the civil strife and uproar, the bloodshed and havoc brought on between the partisans of the Republic and the Carlists in Spain.

117   Only too many such instances are available to demonstrate the fact that Europe is morally un-

civilized. Since the writer has no wish to cast aspersions on anyone He has confined Himself to these few examples. It is clear that no perceptive and well-informed mind can countenance such events. Is it right and proper that peoples among whom, diametrically opposed to the most desirable human behavior, such horrors take place, should dare lay claim to a real and adequate civilization? Especially when out of all this no results can be hoped for except the winning of a transient victory; and since this outcome never endures, it is, to the wise, not worth the effort.

Time and again down the centuries, the German state has subdued the French; over and over, the kingdom of France has governed German land. Is it permissible that in our day 600,000 helpless creatures should be offered up as a sacrifice to such nominal and temporary uses and results? No, by the Lord God! Even a child can see the evil of it. Yet the pursuit of passion and desire will wrap the eyes in a thousand veils that rise out of the heart to blind the sight and the insight as well. 118

Desire and self come in the door 119
And blot out virtue, bright before,

And a hundred veils will rise
From the heart, to blind the eyes.[42]

120   True civilization will unfurl its banner in the midmost heart of the world whenever a certain number of its distinguished and high-minded sovereigns—the shining exemplars of devotion and determination—shall, for the good and happiness of all mankind, arise, with firm resolve and clear vision, to establish the Cause of Universal Peace. They must make the Cause of Peace the object of general consultation, and seek by every means in their power to establish a Union of the nations of the world. They must conclude a binding treaty and establish a covenant, the provisions of which shall be sound, inviolable and definite. They must proclaim it to all the world and obtain for it the sanction of all the human race. This supreme and noble undertaking—the real source of the peace and well-being of all the world—should be regarded as sacred by all that dwell on earth. All the forces of humanity must be mobilized to ensure the stability and permanence of this Most Great Covenant. In this all-embracing

---

42. Rúmí, The *Mathnavi*, I, 334.

Pact the limits and frontiers of each and every nation should be clearly fixed, the principles underlying the relations of governments towards one another definitely laid down, and all international agreements and obligations ascertained. In like manner, the size of the armaments of every government should be strictly limited, for if the preparations for war and the military forces of any nation should be allowed to increase, they will arouse the suspicion of others. The fundamental principle underlying this solemn Pact should be so fixed that if any government later violate any one of its provisions, all the governments on earth should arise to reduce it to utter submission, nay the human race as a whole should resolve, with every power at its disposal, to destroy that government. Should this greatest of all remedies be applied to the sick body of the world, it will assuredly recover from its ills and will remain eternally safe and secure.[43]

---

43. The foregoing paragraph, together with the later paragraph beginning "A few, unaware of the power latent in human endeavor," was translated by Shoghi Effendi, Guardian of the Bahá'í Faith. Cf. *The World Order of Bahá'u'lláh*, pp. 37–38.

121 Observe that if such a happy situation be forth-coming, no government would need continually to pile up the weapons of war, nor feel itself obliged to produce ever new military weapons with which to conquer the human race. A small force for the purposes of internal security, the correction of criminal and disorderly elements and the prevention of local disturbances, would be required—no more. In this way the entire population would, first of all, be relieved of the crushing burden of expenditure currently imposed for military purposes, and secondly, great numbers of people would cease to devote their time to the continual devising of new weapons of destruction—those testimonials of greed and blood-thirstiness, so inconsistent with the gift of life—and would instead bend their efforts to the production of whatever will foster human existence and peace and well-being, and would become the cause of universal development and prosperity. Then every nation on earth will reign in honor, and every people will be cradled in tranquillity and content.

122 A few, unaware of the power latent in human endeavor, consider this matter as highly imprac-ticable, nay even beyond the scope of man's ut-

most efforts. Such is not the case, however. On the contrary, thanks to the unfailing grace of God, the loving-kindness of His favored ones, the unrivaled endeavors of wise and capable souls, and the thoughts and ideas of the peerless leaders of this age, nothing whatsoever can be regarded as unattainable. Endeavor, ceaseless endeavor, is required. Nothing short of an indomitable determination can possibly achieve it. Many a cause which past ages have regarded as purely visionary, yet in this day has become most easy and practicable. Why should this most great and lofty Cause—the daystar of the firmament of true civilization and the cause of the glory, the advancement, the well-being and the success of all humanity—be regarded as impossible of achievement? Surely the day will come when its beauteous light shall shed illumination upon the assemblage of man.

The apparatus of conflict will, as preparations go on at their present rate, reach the point where war will become something intolerable to mankind. 123

87

124   It is clear from what has already been said that man's glory and greatness do not consist in his being avid for blood and sharp of claw, in tearing down cities and spreading havoc, in butchering armed forces and civilians. What would mean a bright future for him would be his reputation for justice, his kindness to the entire population whether high or low, his building up countries and cities, villages and districts, his making life easy, peaceful and happy for his fellow beings, his laying down fundamental principles for progress, his raising the standards and increasing the wealth of the entire population.

125   Consider how throughout history many a king has sat on his throne as a conqueror. Among them were Hulágú Khán and Tamerlane, who took over the vast continent of Asia, and Alexander of Macedon and Napoleon I, who stretched their arrogant fists over three of the earth's five continents. And what was gained by all their mighty victories? Was any country made to flourish, did any happiness result, did any throne stand? Or was it rather that those reigning houses lost their power? Except that Asia went up in the flame of many battles and fell away to ashes, Changíz's Hulágú, the warlord, gathered no fruit from all

his conquests. And Tamerlane, out of all his triumphs, reaped only the peoples blown to the winds, and universal ruin. And Alexander had nothing to show for his vast victories, except that his son toppled from the throne and Philip and Ptolemy took over the dominions he once had ruled. And what did the first Napoleon gain from subjugating the kings of Europe, except the destruction of flourishing countries, the downfall of their inhabitants, the spreading of terror and anguish across Europe and, at the end of his days, his own captivity? So much for the conquerors and the monuments they leave behind them.

Contrast with this the praiseworthy qualities and the greatness and nobility of Anúshírván the Generous and the Just.[44] That fair-minded monarch came to power at a time when the once solidly established throne of Persia was about to crumble away. With his divine gift of intellect, he laid the foundations of justice, uprooting oppression and tyranny and gathering the scattered peoples of Persia under the wings of his dominion. Thanks to the restoring influence of his con-

126

---

44. Sásáníyán king who reigned 531–578 A.D.

tinual care, Persia that had lain withered and desolate was quickened into life and rapidly changed into the fairest of all flourishing nations. He rebuilt and reinforced the disorganized powers of the state, and the renown of his righteousness and justice echoed across the seven climes,[45] until the peoples rose up out of their degradation and misery to the heights of felicity and honor. Although he was a Magian, Muḥammad, that Center of creation and Sun of prophethood, said of him: "I was born in the time of a just king," and rejoiced at having come into the world during his reign. Did this illustrious personage achieve his exalted station by virtue of his admirable qualities or rather by reaching out to conquer the earth and spill the blood of its peoples? Observe that he attained to such a distinguished rank in the heart of the world that his greatness still rings out through all the impermanence of time, and he won eternal life. Should We comment on the continuing life of the great, this brief essay would be unduly prolonged, and since it is by no means certain that public opinion in Persia will be mate-

---

45. i.e., the whole world.

rially affected by its perusal, We shall abridge the work, and go on to other matters which come within the purview of the public mind. If, however, it develops that this abridgement produces favorable results, We shall, God willing, write a number of books dealing at length and usefully with fundamental principles of the divine wisdom in its relation to the phenomenal world.

No power on earth can prevail against 127 the armies of justice, and every citadel must fall before them; for men willingly go down under the triumphant strokes of this decisive blade, and desolate places bloom and flourish under the tramplings of this host. There are two mighty banners which, when they cast their shadow across the crown of any king, will cause the influence of his government quickly and easily to penetrate the whole earth, even as if it were the light of the sun: the first of these two banners is wisdom; the second is justice.

Against these two most potent forces, the iron hills cannot prevail, and Alexander's wall will break before them. It is clear that life in this fast-fading world is as fleeting and inconstant as the morning wind, and this being so, how fortunate are the great who leave a good name behind them, and the memory of a lifetime spent in the pathway of the good pleasure of God.

128   *It is all one, if it be a throne*
      Or the bare ground under the open sky,
      Where the pure soul lays him
      Down to die.[46]

129   A conquest can be a praiseworthy thing, and there are times when war becomes the powerful basis of peace, and ruin the very means of reconstruction. If, for example, a high-minded sovereign marshals his troops to block the onset of the insurgent and the aggressor, or again, if he takes the field and distinguishes himself in a struggle to unify a divided state and people, if, in brief, he

---

46. Saʻdí, The *Gulistán*, On the Conduct of Kings.

is waging war for a righteous purpose, then this seeming wrath is mercy itself, and this apparent tyranny the very substance of justice and this warfare the cornerstone of peace. Today, the task befitting great rulers is to establish universal peace, for in this lies the freedom of all peoples.

The fourth phrase of the aforementioned Utterance which points out the way of salvation is: "obedient to the commandments of his Lord." It is certain that man's highest distinction is to be lowly before and obedient to his God; that his greatest glory, his most exalted rank and honor, depend on his close observance of the divine commands and prohibitions. Religion is the light of the world, and the progress, achievement, and happiness of man result from obedience to the laws set down in the holy Books. Briefly, it is demonstrable that in this life, both outwardly and inwardly the mightiest of structures, the most solidly

130

established, the most enduring, standing guard over the world, assuring both the spiritual and the material perfections of mankind, and protecting the happiness and the civilization of society—is religion.

131   It is true that there are foolish individuals who have never properly examined the fundamentals of the divine religions, who have taken as their criterion the behavior of a few religious hypocrites and measured all religious persons by that yardstick, and have on this account concluded that religions are an obstacle to progress, a divisive factor and a cause of malevolence and enmity among peoples. They have not even observed this much, that the principles of the divine religions can hardly be evaluated by the acts of those who only claim to follow them. For every excellent thing, peerless though it may be, can still be diverted to the wrong ends. A lighted lamp in the hands of an ignorant child or of the blind will not dispel the surrounding darkness nor light up the house— it will set both the bearer and the house on fire. Can we, in such an instance, blame the lamp? No, by the Lord God! To the seeing, a lamp is a guide and will show him his path; but it is a disaster to the blind.

Among those who have repudiated religious   132
faith was the Frenchman, Voltaire, who wrote a
great number of books attacking the religions,
works which are no better than children's play-
things. This individual, taking as his criterion
the omissions and commissions of the Pope, the
head of the Roman Catholic religion, and the in-
trigues and quarrels of the spiritual leaders of
Christendom, opened his mouth and caviled at
the Spirit of God (Jesus). In the unsoundness of
his reasoning, he failed to grasp the true significance of the sacred Scriptures, took exception
to certain portions of the revealed Texts and dwelt
on the difficulties involved. "And We send down
of the Qur'án that which is a healing and a mercy
to the faithful: But it shall only add to the ruin of
the wicked."[47]

> *The Sage of Ghazna*[48] *told the mystic story*   133
> *To his veiled hearers, in an allegory:*
> *If those who err see naught in the Qur'án*
> *But only words, it's not to wonder on;*

---

47. Qur'án 17:84.
48. The poet Saná'í.

Of all the sun's fire, lighting up the sky
Only the warmth can reach a blind man's
eye.[49]

134   "Many will He mislead by such parables and many guide: but none will He mislead thereby except the wicked . . ."[50]

135   It is certain that the greatest of instrumentalities for achieving the advancement and the glory of man, the supreme agency for the enlightenment and the redemption of the world, is love and fellowship and unity among all the members of the human race. Nothing can be effected in the world, not even conceivably, without unity and agreement, and the perfect means for engendering fellowship and union is true religion. "Hadst Thou spent all the riches of the earth, Thou couldst not have united their hearts; but God hath united them . . ."[51]

136   With the advent of the Prophets of God, their power of creating a real union, one which is both

---

49. Rúmí, The *Mathnaví*, III, 4229–4231.
50. Qur'án 2:24.
51. Qur'án 8:64.

external and of the heart, draws together malevolent peoples who have been thirsting for one another's blood, into the one shelter of the Word of God. Then a hundred thousand souls become as one soul, and unnumbered individuals emerge as one body.

> Once they were as the waves of the sea 137
> That the wind made many out of one.
> Then God shed down on them His sun,
> And His sun but one can never be.
> Souls of dogs and wolves go separately,
> But the soul of the lions of God is one.[52]

The events that transpired at the advent of the 138 Prophets of the past, and Their ways and works and circumstances, are not adequately set down in authoritative histories, and are referred to only

---

52. See Rúmí, The *Mathnaví*, II, 185 and 189. Also the Ḥadíth: "God created the creatures in darkness, then He sprinkled some of His Light upon them. Those whom some of that Light reached took the right way, while those whom it missed wandered from the straight road." Cf. R. A. Nicholson's "The Mathnawí of Jalálu'ddín Rúmí" in the E. J. W. Gibb Memorial Series.

in condensed form in the verses of the Qur'án, the Holy Traditions and the Torah. Since, however, all events from the days of Moses until the present time are contained in the mighty Qur'án, the authoritative Traditions, the Torah and other reliable sources, We shall content Ourself with brief references here, the purpose being to determine conclusively whether religion is the very basis and root-principle of culture and civilization, or whether as Voltaire and his like suppose, it defeats all social progress, well-being and peace.

139   To preclude once and for all objections on the part of any of the world's peoples, We shall conduct Our discussion conformably to those authoritative accounts which all nations are agreed upon.

140   At a time when the Israelites had multiplied in Egypt and were spread throughout the whole country, the Coptic Pharaohs of Egypt determined to strengthen and favor their own Coptic peoples and to degrade and dishonor the children of Israel, whom they regarded as foreigners. Over a long period, the Israelites, divided and scattered, were captive in the hands of the tyrannical Copts, and were scorned and despised by all, so that the meanest of the Copts would freely persecute and lord it over the noblest of the Israelites. The en-

slavement, wretchedness and helplessness of the Hebrews reached such a pitch that they were never, day or night, secure in their own persons nor able to provide any defense for their wives and families against the tyranny of their Pharaohic captors. Then their food was the fragments of their own broken hearts, and their drink a river of tears. They continued on in this anguish until suddenly Moses, the All-Beauteous, beheld the divine Light streaming out of the blessed Vale, the place that was holy ground, and heard the quickening voice of God as it spoke from the flame of that Tree "neither of the East nor of the West,"[53] and He stood up in the full panoply of His universal prophethood. In the midst of the Israelites, He blazed out like a lamp of divine guidance, and by the light of salvation He led that lost people out of the shadows of ignorance into knowledge and perfection. He gathered Israel's scattered tribes into the shelter of the unifying and universal Word of God, and over the heights of union He raised up the banner of harmony, so that within a brief interval those benighted souls became spiritually educated, and they who had been strangers to the

---

53. Qur'án 24:35.

truth, rallied to the cause of the oneness of God, and were delivered out of their wretchedness, their indigence, their incomprehension and captivity and achieved a supreme degree of happiness and honor. They emigrated from Egypt, set out for Israel's original homeland, and came to Canaan and Philistia. They first conquered the shores of the River Jordan, and Jericho, and settled in that area, and ultimately all the neighboring regions, such as Phoenicia, Edom and Ammon, came under their sway. In Joshua's time there were thirty-one governments in the hands of the Israelites, and in every noble human attribute—learning, stability, determination, courage, honor, generosity—this people came to surpass all the nations of the earth. When in those days an Israelite would enter a gathering, he was immediately singled out for his many virtues, and even foreign peoples wishing to praise a man would say that he was like an Israelite.

141   It is furthermore a matter of record in numerous historical works that the philosophers of Greece such as Pythagoras, acquired the major part of their philosophy, both divine and material, from the disciples of Solomon. And Socrates after having eagerly journeyed to meet with some

of Israel's most illustrious scholars and divines, on his return to Greece established the concept of the oneness of God and the continuing life of the human soul after it has put off its elemental dust. Ultimately, the ignorant among the Greeks denounced this man who had fathomed the inmost mysteries of wisdom, and rose up to take his life; and then the populace forced the hand of their ruler, and in council assembled they caused Socrates to drink from the poisoned cup.

After the Israelites had advanced along every 142 level of civilization, and had achieved success in the highest possible degree, they began little by little to forget the root-principles of the Mosaic law and Faith, to busy themselves with rites and ceremonials and to show forth unbecoming conduct. In the days of Rehoboam, the son of Solomon, terrible dissension broke out among them; one of their number, Jeroboam, plotted to get the throne, and it was he who introduced the worship of idols. The strife between Rehoboam and Jeroboam led to centuries of warfare between their descendants, with the result that the tribes of Israel were scattered and disrupted. In brief, it was because they forgot the meaning of the law of God that they became involved in ignorant fanaticism and blameworthy practices such as insurgence and sedition. Their divines, having concluded that all those essential qualifications of humankind set forth in the Holy Book were by then a dead letter, began to think only of furthering their own selfish interests, and afflicted the people by allowing them to sink into the lowest depths of heedlessness and ignorance. And the fruit of their wrong doing was this, that the oldtime glory which had endured so long now changed to degradation, and the rulers of Persia, of Greece, and of Rome, took them over. The banners of their sovereignty were reversed; the ignorance, foolishness, abasement and self-love of their religious leaders and their scholars were brought to light in the coming of Nebuchadnezzar, King of Babylon, who destroyed them. After a general massacre, and the sacking and razing of their houses and even the uprooting of their trees, he took captive whatever remnants his sword had spared and carried them off to Babylon. Seventy years later the descendants of these captives were released and went back to Jerusalem. Then Hezekiah and Ezra reestablished in their midst the fundamental principles of the Holy Book, and day by day the Israelites advanced, and the morning-brightness of their earlier ages dawned again. In a short time, however, great dissensions as to belief and conduct broke out anew, and again the one concern of the Jewish doctors became the promotion of their own selfish purposes, and the reforms that had obtained in Ezra's time were changed to perversity and corruption. The situation worsened to such a degree that time and again, the armies of the republic of Rome and of its rulers conquered Israelite territory. Finally the warlike Titus, commander of the Roman forces, trampled the Jewish homeland into dust, putting every man to the sword, taking the women and children captive, flattening their houses, tearing out their trees, burning their books, looting their treasures, and reducing Jerusalem and the Temple to an ash heap. After this supreme calamity, the star of Israel's dominion sank away to nothing, and to this day, the remnant of that vanished nation has been scattered to the four winds. "Humiliation and misery were stamped upon them."[54] These two most great afflictions, brought on by Nebuchadnezzar and Titus, are referred to in the glorious Qur'án: "And We solemnly declared to

---

54. Qur'án 2:58.

the children of Israel in the Book, 'Twice surely will ye commit evil in the earth, and with great loftiness of pride will ye surely be uplifted.' And when the menace for the first of the two came to be executed, We sent against you Our servants endowed with terrible prowess; and they searched the inmost part of your abodes, and the menace was accomplished . . . And when the punishment threatened for your latter transgression came to be inflicted, then We sent an enemy to sadden your faces, and to enter the Temple as they entered it at first, and to destroy with utter destruction that which they had conquered."[55]

143   Our purpose is to show how true religion promotes the civilization and honor, the prosperity and prestige, the learning and advancement of a people once abject, enslaved and ignorant, and how, when it falls into the hands of religious leaders who are foolish and fanatical, it is diverted to the wrong ends, until this greatest of splendors turns into blackest night.

144   When for the second time the unmistakable signs of Israel's disintegration, abasement, subjection and annihilation had become apparent,

---

55. Qur'án 17:4 ff.

then the sweet and holy breathings of the Spirit of God (Jesus) were shed across Jordan and the land of Galilee; the cloud of divine pity overspread those skies, and rained down the copious waters of the spirit, and after those swelling showers that came from the most great Sea, the Holy Land put forth its perfume and blossomed with the knowledge of God. Then the solemn Gospel song rose up till it rang in the ears of those who dwell in the chambers of heaven, and at the touch of Jesus' breath the unmindful dead that lay in the graves of their ignorance lifted up their heads to receive eternal life. For the space of three years, that Luminary of perfections walked about the fields of Palestine and in the neighborhood of Jerusalem, leading all men into the dawn of redemption, teaching them how to acquire spiritual qualities and attributes well-pleasing to God. Had the people of Israel believed in that beauteous Countenance, they would have girded themselves to serve and obey Him heart and soul, and through the quickening fragrance of His Spirit they would have regained their lost vitality and gone on to new victories.

Alas, of what avail was it; they turned away 145 and opposed Him. They rose up and tormented that Source of divine knowledge, that Point where the Revelation had come down—all except for a handful who, turning their faces toward God, were cleansed of the stain of this world and found their way to the heights of the placeless Realm. They inflicted every agony on that Wellspring of grace until it became impossible for Him to live in the towns, and still He lifted up the flag of salvation and solidly established the fundamentals of human righteousness, that essential basis of true civilization.

146 In the fifth chapter of Matthew beginning with the thirty-seventh verse He counsels: "Resist not evil and injury with its like; but whosoever shall smite thee on thy right cheek, turn to him the other also." And further, from the forty-third verse: "Ye have heard that it hath been said, 'Thou shalt love thy neighbor, and thou shalt not vex thine enemy with enmity.'[56] But I say unto you,

---

56. The King James Bible reads: "Ye have heard that it hath been said, Thou shalt love thy neighbour, and hate thine enemy." Scholars object to this reading because it is contrary to the known Law as set forth in Leviticus 19:18, Exodus 23:4–5, Proverbs 25:21, the Talmud, etc.

love your enemies, bless them that curse you, do good to them that hate you, and pray for them which despitefully use you, and persecute you; that ye may be the children of your Father which is in heaven: for He maketh His sun to rise on the evil and on the good, and sendeth down the rain of His mercy on the just and on the unjust. For if ye love them which love you, what reward have ye? Do not even the publicans the same?"

Many were the counsels of this kind that were uttered by that Dayspring of divine wisdom, and souls who have become characterized with such attributes of holiness are the distilled essence of creation and the sources of true civilization. 147

Jesus, then, founded the sacred law on a basis of moral character and complete spirituality, and for those who believed in Him He delineated a special way of life which constitutes the highest type of action on earth. And while those emblems of redemption were to outward seeming abandoned to the malevolence and persecution of their tormentors, in reality they had been delivered out of the hopeless darkness which encompassed the Jews and they shone forth in everlasting glory at the dawn of that new day. 148

149   That mighty Jewish nation toppled and crumbled away, but those few souls who sought shelter beneath the Messianic Tree transformed all human life. At that time the peoples of the world were utterly ignorant, fanatical and idolatrous. Only a small group of Jews professed belief in the oneness of God and they were wretched outcasts. These holy Christian souls now stood up to promulgate a Cause which was diametrically opposed and repugnant to the beliefs of the entire human race. The kings of four out of the world's five continents inexorably resolved to wipe out the followers of Christ, and nevertheless in the end most of them set about promoting the Faith of God with their whole hearts; all the nations of Europe, many of the peoples of Asia and Africa, and some of the inhabitants of the islands of the Pacific, were gathered into the shelter of the oneness of God.

150   Consider whether there exists anywhere in creation a principle mightier in every sense than religion, or whether any conceivable power is more pervasive than the various divine Faiths, or whether any agency can bring about real love and fellowship and union among all peoples as can belief in an almighty and all-knowing God, or

whether except for the laws of God there has been any evidence of an instrumentality for educating all mankind in every phase of righteousness.

Those qualities which the philosophers attained 151 when they had reached the very heights of their wisdom, those noble human attributes which characterized them at the peak of their perfection, would be exemplified by the believers as soon as they accepted the Faith. Observe how those souls who drank the living waters of redemption at the gracious hands of Jesus, the Spirit of God, and came into the sheltering shade of the Gospel, attained to such a high plane of moral conduct that Galen, the celebrated physician, although not himself a Christian, in his summary of Plato's Republic extolled their actions. A literal translation of his words is as follows:

"The generality of mankind are unable to grasp 152 a sequence of logical arguments. For this reason they stand in need of symbols and parables telling of rewards and punishments in the next world. A confirmatory evidence of this is that today we observe a people called Christians, who believe devoutly in rewards and punishments in a future state. This group show forth excellent actions, similar to the actions of an individual who is a true philosopher. For example, we all see with our own eyes that they have no fear of death, and their passion for justice and fair-dealing is so great that they should be considered true philosophers."[57]

153   The station of a philosopher, in that age and in the mind of Galen, was superior to any other station in the world. Consider then how the enlightening and spiritualizing power of divine religions impels the believers to such heights of perfection that a philosopher like Galen, not himself a Christian, offers such testimony.

154   One demonstration of the excellent character of the Christians in those days was their dedication to charity and good works, and the fact that they founded hospitals and philanthropic institutions. For example, the first person to establish public clinics throughout the Roman Empire where the poor, the injured and the helpless re-

---

57. Cf. 'Abdu'l-Bahá, *Some Answered Questions*, ch. LXXXIV, and *Promulgation of Universal Peace*, p. 385. See also *Galen on Jews and Christians* by Richard Walzer, Oxford University Press, 1949, p. 15. The author states that Galen's summary here referred to is lost, being preserved only in Arabic quotations.

ceived medical care, was the Emperor Constantine. This great king was the first Roman ruler to champion the Cause of Christ. He spared no efforts, dedicating his life to the promotion of the principles of the Gospel, and he solidly established the Roman government, which in reality had been nothing but a system of unrelieved oppression, on moderation and justice. His blessed name shines out across the dawn of history like the morning star, and his rank and fame among the world's noblest and most highly civilized is still on the tongues of Christians of all denominations.

What a firm foundation of excellent character 155 was laid down in those days, thanks to the training of holy souls who arose to promote the teachings of the Gospel. How many primary schools, colleges, hospitals, were established, and institutions where fatherless and indigent children received their education. How many were the individuals who sacrificed their own personal advantages and "out of desire to please the Lord"[58] devoted the days of their lives to teaching the masses.

---

58. From Qur'án 4:114; 2:207, etc.

156   When, however, the time approached for the effulgent beauty of Muḥammad to dawn upon the world, the control of Christian affairs passed into the hands of ignorant priests. Those heavenly breezes, soft-flowing from the regions of divine grace, died away, and the laws of the great Evangel, the rock-foundation on which the civilization of the world was based, turned barren of results, this out of misuse and because of the conduct of persons who, seemingly fair, were yet inwardly foul.

157   The noted historians of Europe, in describing the conditions, manners, politics, learning and culture, in all their aspects, of early, medieval and modern times, unanimously record that during the ten centuries constituting the Middle Ages, from the beginning of the sixth century of the Christian era till the close of the fifteenth, Europe was in every respect and to an extreme degree, barbaric and dark. The principal cause of this was that the monks, referred to by European peoples as spiritual and religious leaders, had given up the abiding glory that comes from obedience to the sacred commandments and heavenly teachings of the Gospel, and had joined forces with

the presumptuous and tyrannical rulers of the temporal governments of those times. They had turned their eyes away from everlasting glory, and were devoting all their efforts to the furtherance of their mutual worldly interests and passing and perishable advantages. Ultimately things reached a point where the masses were hopeless prisoners in the hands of these two groups, and all this brought down in ruins the whole structure of the religion, culture, welfare and civilization of the peoples of Europe.

When the unworthy acts and thoughts and the 158 discreditable purposes of the leaders had stilled the sweet savors of the Spirit of God (Jesus) and they ceased to stream across the world, and the darkness of ignorance and bigotry and of actions that were displeasing to God, encompassed the earth, then the dawn of hope shone out and the divine spring drew on; a cloud of mercy overspread the world, and out of the regions of grace the fecund winds began to blow. In the sign of Muḥammad, the Sun of Truth rose over Yathrib (Medina) and the Ḥijáz and cast across the universe the lights of eternal glory. Then the earth of human potentialities was transformed, and the words "The earth shall shine with the light of her Lord,"[59] were fulfilled. The old world turned new again, and its dead body rose into abundant life. Then tyranny and ignorance were overthrown, and towering palaces of knowledge and justice were reared in their place. A sea of enlightenment thundered, and science cast down its rays. The savage peoples of the Ḥijáz, before that Flame of supreme Prophethood was lit in the lamp of Mecca, were the most brutish and benighted of all the peoples of the earth. In all the histories, their depraved and vicious practices, their ferocity and their constant feuds, are a matter of record. In those days the civilized peoples of the world did not even consider the Arab tribes of Mecca and Medina as human beings. And yet, after the Light of the World rose over them, they were— because of the education bestowed on them by that Mine of perfections, that Focal Center of Revelation, and the blessings vouchsafed by the divine law—within a brief interval gathered into the shelter of the principle of divine oneness. This brutish people then attained such a high degree of human perfection and civilization that all

___

59. Qur'án 39:69.

their contemporaries marveled at them. Those very peoples who had always mocked the Arabs and held them up to ridicule as a breed devoid of judgment, now eagerly sought them out, visiting their countries to acquire enlightenment and culture, technical skills, statecraft, arts and sciences.

Observe the influence on material situations 159
of that training which is inculcated by the true Educator. Here were tribes so benighted and untamed that during the period of the Jáhilíyyih they would bury their seven-year-old daughters alive—an act which even an animal, let alone a human being, would hate and shrink from but which they in their extreme degradation considered the ultimate expression of honor and devotion to principle—and this darkened people, thanks to the manifest teachings of that great Personage, advanced to such a degree that after they conquered Egypt, Syria and its capital Damascus, Chaldea, Mesopotamia and Írán, they came to administer single-handedly whatever matters were of major importance in four main regions of the globe.

The Arabs then excelled all the peoples of the 160
world in science and the arts, in industry and invention, in philosophy, government and moral character. And truly, the rise of this brutish and

despicable element, in such a short interval, to the supreme heights of human perfection, is the greatest demonstration of the rightfulness of the Lord Muḥammad's Prophethood.

161   In the early ages of Islám the peoples of Europe acquired the sciences and arts of civilization from Islám as practiced by the inhabitants of Andalusia. A careful and thorough investigation of the historical record will establish the fact that the major part of the civilization of Europe is derived from Islám; for all the writings of Muslim scholars and divines and philosophers were gradually collected in Europe and were with the most painstaking care weighed and debated at academic gatherings and in the centers of learning, after which their valued contents would be put to use. Today, numerous copies of the works of Muslim scholars which are not to be found in Islamic countries, are available in the libraries of Europe. Furthermore, the laws and principles current in all European countries are derived to a considerable degree and indeed virtually in their entirety from the works on jurisprudence and the legal decision of Muslim theologians. Were it not for the fear of unduly lengthening the present text, We would cite these borrowings one by one.

The beginnings of European civilization date 162
from the seventh century of the Muslim era. The
particulars were these: toward the end of the fifth
century of the hegira, the Pope or Head of
Christendom set up a great hue and cry over the
fact that places sacred to the Christians, such as
Jerusalem, Bethlehem and Nazareth, had fallen
under Muslim rule, and he stirred up the kings
and the commoners of Europe to undertake what
he considered a holy war. His impassioned out-
cry waxed so loud that all the countries of Europe responded, and crusading kings at the head
of innumerable hosts passed over the Sea of
Marmara and made their way to the continent of
Asia. In those days the Fátimid caliphs ruled over
Egypt and some countries of the West, and most
of the time the kings of Syria, that is the Saljúqs,
were subject to them as well. Briefly, the kings of
the West with their unnumbered armies fell upon
Syria and Egypt, and there was continuous warfare between the Syrian rulers and those of Europe for a period of two hundred and three years.
Reinforcements were always coming in from Europe, and time and time again the Western rulers
stormed and took over every castle in Syria, and
as often, the kings of Islám delivered them out of

their hands. Finally Saladin, in the year 693 A.H., drove the European kings and their armies out of Egypt and off the Syrian coast. Hopelessly beaten, they went back to Europe. In the course of these wars of the Crusades, millions of human beings perished. To sum up, from 490 A.H. until 693, kings, commanders and other European leaders continually came and went between Egypt, Syria and the West, and when in the end they all returned home, they introduced into Europe whatever they had observed over two hundred and odd years in Muslim countries as to government, social development and learning, colleges, schools and the refinements of living. The civilization of Europe dates from that time.

163   O people of Persia! How long will your torpor and lethargy last? You were once the lords of the whole earth; the world was at your beck and call. How is it that your glory has lapsed and you have fallen from favor

now, and crept away into some corner of oblivion? You were the fountainhead of learning, the unfailing spring of light for all the earth, how is it that you are withered now, and quenched, and faint of heart? You who once lit the world, how is it that you lurk, inert, bemused, in darkness now? Open your mind's eye, see your great and present need. Rise up and struggle, seek education, seek enlightenment. Is it meet that a foreign people should receive from your own forbears its culture and its knowledge, and that you, their blood, their rightful heirs, should go without? How does it seem, when your neighbors are at work by day and night with their whole hearts, providing for their advancement, their honor and prosperity, that you, in your ignorant fanaticism, are busy only with your quarrels and antipathies, your indulgences and appetites and empty dreams? Is it commendable that you should waste and fritter away in apathy the brilliance that is your birthright, your native competence, your inborn understanding? Again, We have digressed from Our theme.

164 Those European intellectuals who are well-informed as to the facts of Europe's past, and are characterized by truthfulness and a sense of justice, unanimously acknowledge that in every particular the basic elements of their civilization are derived from Islám. For example Draper,[60] the well-known French authority, a writer whose accuracy, ability

---

60. The Persian text transliterates this author's name as "Draybár" and titles his work *The Progress of Peoples*. The reference is apparently to John William Draper, 1811–1882, celebrated chemist and widely-translated historian. Detailed material on Muslim contributions to the West, and on Gerbert (Pope Sylvester II) appears in the second volume of the work cited. Of some of Europe's systematically unacknowledged obligations to Islám the author writes: "Injustice founded on religious rancour and national conceit cannot be perpetuated for ever." (Vol. II, p. 42, Rev. ed.) The *Dictionary of American Biography* states that Draper's father was a Roman Catholic who assumed the name John Christopher Draper when disowned by his family for becoming a Methodist, and that his real name is unknown. The translator is indebted to Mr. Paul North Rice, Chief of the New York Public Library's Reference Department, for the information that available data on Draper's family history and nationality are in conflict; *The Drapers in America* by Thomas Waln-Morgan (1892) states that Draper's father was

and learning are attested by all European scholars, in one of his best-known works, *The Intellectual Development of Europe,* has written a detailed account in this connection, that is, with reference to the derivation by the peoples of Europe of the fundamentals of civilization and the bases of progress and well-being from Islám. His account is exhaustive, and a translation here would unduly lengthen out the present work and would indeed be irrelevant to Our purpose. If further details are desired the reader may refer to that text.

In essence, the author shows how the totality 165 of Europe's civilization—its laws, principles, institutions, its sciences, philosophies, varied learning, its civilized manners and customs, its literature, art and industry, its organization, its

---

born in London, while Albert E. Henschel in "Centenary of John William Draper" (New York University "Colonnade," June, 1911) has the following: "If there be among us any who trace their lineage to the sunny fields of Italy, they may feel a just pride in John William Draper, for his father, John C. Draper, was an Italian by birth . . ." The translator's thanks are also due to Madame Laura Dreyfus-Barney for investigations in connection with this passage at the Library of Congress and the Bibliothéque Nationale.

discipline, its behavior, its commendable character traits, and even many of the words current in
the French language, derives from the Arabs. One
by one, he investigates each of these elements in
detail, even giving the period when each was
brought over from Islám. He describes as well the
arrival of the Arabs in the West, in what is now
Spain, and how in a short time they established a
well-developed civilization there, and to what a
high degree of excellence their administrative system and scholarship attained, and how solidly
founded and well regulated were their schools and
colleges, where sciences and philosophy, arts and
crafts, were taught; what a high level of leadership they achieved in the arts of civilization and
how many were the children of Europe's leading
families who were sent to attend the schools of
Cordova and Granada, Seville and Toledo to acquire the sciences and arts of civilized life. He
even records that a European named Gerbert came
to the West and enrolled at the University of
Cordova in Arab territory, studied arts and sciences there, and after his return to Europe
achieved such prominence that ultimately he was
elevated to the leadership of the Catholic Church
and became the Pope.

The purpose of these references is to establish 166
the fact that the religions of God are the true
source of the spiritual and material perfections
of man, and the fountainhead for all mankind of
enlightenment and beneficial knowledge. If one
observes the matter justly it will be found that all
the laws of politics are contained in these few and
holy words:

"And they enjoin what is just, and forbid what 167
is unjust, and speed on in good works. These are
of the righteous."[61] And again: "that there may be
among you a people who invite to the good, and
enjoin the just, and forbid the wrong. These are
they with whom it shall be well."[62] And further:
"Verily, God enjoineth justice and the doing of
good . . . and He forbiddeth wickedness and oppression. He warneth you that haply ye may be
mindful."[63] And yet again, of the civilizing of
human behavior: "Make due allowances; and enjoin what is just, and withdraw from the ignorant."[64] And likewise: ". . . who master their an-

61. Qur'án 3:110.
62. Qur'án 3:100.
63. Qur'án 16:92.
64. Qur'án 7:198.

123

ger, and forgive others! God loveth the doers of good."[65] And again: "There is no righteousness in turning your faces toward the East or the West, but he is righteous who believeth in God, and the last day, and the angels, and the Scriptures, and the Prophets; who for the love of God disburseth his wealth to his kindred, and to orphans, and the needy and the wayfarer, and those who ask, and for ransom; who observeth prayer, and payeth the legal alms, and who is of those who perform their covenant when they have covenanted, and are patient under ills and hardships, and in time of trouble: these are they who are just, and these are they who fear the Lord."[66] And yet further: "They prefer them before themselves, though poverty be their own lot."[67] See how these few sacred verses encompass the highest levels and innermost meanings of civilization and embody all the excellencies of human character.

168   By the Lord God, and there is no God but He, even the minutest details of civilized life derive

---

65. Qur'án 3:128.
66. Qur'án 2:172.
67. Qur'án 59:9.

from the grace of the Prophets of God. What thing of value to mankind has ever come into being which was not first set forth either directly or by implication in the Holy Scriptures?

Alas, of what avail is it. When the weapons are 169 in cowards' hands, no man's life and property are safe, and thieves only grow the stronger. When, in the same way, a far-from-perfect priesthood acquire control of affairs, they come down like a massive curtain between the people and the light of Faith.

Sincerity is the foundation-stone of faith. That 170 is, a religious individual must disregard his personal desires and seek in whatever way he can wholeheartedly to serve the public interest; and it is impossible for a human being to turn aside from his own selfish advantages and sacrifice his own good for the good of the community except through true religious faith. For self-love is kneaded into the very clay of man, and it is not possible that, without any hope of a substantial reward, he should neglect his own present material good. That individual, however, who puts his faith in God and believes in the words of God—because he is promised and certain of a plentiful reward in the next life, and because worldly benefits as compared to the abiding joy and glory of future planes of existence are nothing to him—will for the sake of God abandon his own peace and profit and will freely consecrate his heart and soul to the common good. "A man, too, there is who selleth his very self out of desire to please God."[68]

171   There are some who imagine that an innate sense of human dignity will prevent man from committing evil actions and insure his spiritual and material perfection. That is, that an individual who is characterized with natural intelligence, high resolve, and a driving zeal, will, without any consideration for the severe punishments consequent on evil acts, or for the great rewards of righteousness, instinctively refrain from inflicting harm on his fellow men and will hunger and thirst to do good. And yet, if we ponder the lessons of history it will become evident that this very sense of honor and dignity is itself one of the bounties deriving from the instructions of the Prophets of God. We also observe in infants the signs of aggression and lawlessness, and that if a child is

---

68. Qur'án 2:203.

deprived of a teacher's instructions his undesirable qualities increase from one moment to the next. It is therefore clear that the emergence of this natural sense of human dignity and honor is the result of education. Secondly, even if we grant for the sake of the argument that instinctive intelligence and an innate moral quality would prevent wrongdoing, it is obvious that individuals so characterized are as rare as the philosopher's stone. An assumption of this sort cannot be validated by mere words, it must be supported by the facts. Let us see what power in creation impels the masses toward righteous aims and deeds!

Aside from this, if that rare individual who does 172 exemplify such a faculty should also become an embodiment of the fear of God, it is certain that his strivings toward righteousness would be strongly reinforced.

Universal benefits derive from the grace of the 173 divine religions, for they lead their true followers to sincerity of intent, to high purpose, to purity and spotless honor, to surpassing kindness and compassion, to the keeping of their covenants when they have covenanted, to concern for the rights of others, to liberality, to justice in every aspect of life, to humanity and philanthropy, to valor and to unflagging efforts in the service of mankind. It is religion, to sum up, which produces all human virtues, and it is these virtues which are the bright candles of civilization. If a man is not characterized by these excellent qualities, it is certain that he has never attained to so much as a drop out of the fathomless river of the waters of life that flows through the teachings of the Holy Books, nor caught the faintest breath of the fragrant breezes that blow from the gardens of God; for nothing on earth can be demonstrated by words alone, and every level of existence is known by its signs and symbols, and every degree in man's development has its identifying mark.

174 The purpose of these statements is to make it abundantly clear that the divine religions, the holy precepts, the heavenly teachings, are the unassailable basis of human happiness, and that the peoples of the world can hope for no real relief or deliverance without this one great remedy. This panacea must, however, be administered by a wise and skilled physician, for in the hands of an incompetent all the cures that the Lord of men has ever created to heal men's ills could produce no

health, and would on the contrary only destroy the helpless and burden the hearts of the already afflicted.

That Source of divine wisdom, that Manifestation of Universal Prophethood (Muḥammad), encouraging mankind to acquire sciences and arts and similar advantages has commanded them to seek these even in the furthermost reaches of China; yet the incompetent and caviling doctors forbid this, offering as their justification the saying, "He who imitates a people is one of them." They have not even grasped what is meant by the "imitation" referred to, nor do they know that the divine religions enjoin upon and encourage all the faithful to adopt such principles as will conduce to continuous improvements, and to acquire from other peoples sciences and arts. Whoever expresses himself to the contrary has never drunk of the nectar of knowledge and is astray in his own ignorance, groping after the mirage of his desires.

Judge this aright: which one of these modern developments, whether in themselves or in their application, is contrary to the divine commandments? If they mean the establishment of parliaments, these are enjoined by the very text of

175

176

the holy verse: "and whose affairs are guided by mutual counsel."[69] And again, addressing the Dayspring of all knowledge, the Source of perfection (Muḥammad), in spite of His being in possession of universal wisdom, the words are: "and consult them in the affair."[70] In view of this how can the question of mutual consultation be in conflict with the religious law? The great advantages of consultation can be established by logical arguments as well.

177   Can they say that it would be contrary to the laws of God to make a death sentence conditional on the most careful investigations, on the sanction of numerous bodies, on legal proof and the royal order? Can they claim that what went on under the previous government was in conformity with the Qur'án? For example, in the days when Ḥájí Mírzá Áqásí was Prime Minister, it was heard from many sources that the governor of Gulpáygán seized thirteen defenseless bailiffs of that region, all of them of holy lineage, all of them guiltless, and without a trial, and without obtaining any higher sanction, beheaded them in a single hour.

---

69. Qur'án 42:36.
70. Qur'án 3:153.

At one time the population of Persia exceeded 178 fifty millions. This has been dissipated partly through civil wars, but predominantly because of the lack of an adequate system of government and the despotism and unbridled authority of provincial and local governors. With the passage of time, not one-fifth of the population has survived, for the governors would select any victim they cared to, however innocent, and vent their wrath on him and destroy him. Or, for a whim, they would make a pet out of some proven mass murderer. Not a soul could speak out, because the governor was in absolute control. Can we say that these things were in conformity with justice or with the laws of God?

Can we maintain that it is contrary to the fun- 179 damentals of the Faith to encourage the acquisition of useful arts and of general knowledge, to inform oneself as to the truths of such physical sciences as are beneficial to man, and to widen the scope of industry and increase the products of commerce and multiply the nation's avenues of wealth? Would it conflict with the worship of God to establish law and order in the cities and organize the rural districts, to repair the roads and build railroads and facilitate transportation and travel and thus increase the people's well-being? Would it be inconsistent with the divine commands and prohibitions if we were to work the abandoned mines which are the greatest source of the nation's wealth, and to build factories, from which come the entire people's comfort, security and affluence? Or to stimulate the creation of new industries and to promote improvements in our domestic products?

180   By the All-Glorious! I am astonished to find what a veil has fallen across their eyes, and how it blinds them even to such obvious necessities as these. And there is no doubt whatever that when conclusive arguments and proofs of this sort are advanced, they will answer, out of a thousand hidden spites and prejudices: "On the Day of Judgment, when men stand before their Lord, they will not be questioned as to their education and the degree of their culture—rather will they be examined as to their good deeds." Let us grant this and assume that man will not be asked as to his culture and education; even so, on that great Day of Reckoning, will not the leaders be called to account? Will it not be said to them: "O chiefs and leaders! Why did ye cause this mighty nation to fall from the heights of its former glory, to pass

from its place at the heart and center of the civilized world? Ye were well able to take hold of such measures as would lead to the high honor of this people. This ye failed to do, and ye even went on to deprive them of the common benefits enjoyed by all. Did not this people once shine out like stars in an auspicious heaven? How have ye dared to quench their light in darkness! Ye could have lit the lamp of temporal and eternal glory for them; why did ye fail to strive for this with all your hearts? And when by God's grace a flaming Light flared up, why did ye fail to shelter it in the glass of your valor, from the winds that beat against it? Why did ye rise up in all your might to put it out?"

"And every man's fate have We fastened about his neck: and on the Day of Resurrection will We bring it forth to him a book which shall be proffered to him wide open."[71] 181

Again, is there any deed in the world that would be nobler than service to the common good? Is there any greater blessing conceivable for a man, than that he should become the cause of the edu- 182

---

71. Qur'án 17:14.

cation, the development, the prosperity and honor of his fellow-creatures? No, by the Lord God! The highest righteousness of all is for blessed souls to take hold of the hands of the helpless and deliver them out of their ignorance and abasement and poverty, and with pure motives, and only for the sake of God, to arise and energetically devote themselves to the service of the masses, forgetting their own worldly advantage and working only to serve the general good. "They prefer them before themselves, though poverty be their own lot."[72] "The best of men are those who serve the people; the worst of men are those who harm the people."

183   Glory be to God! What an extraordinary situation now obtains, when no one, hearing a claim advanced, asks himself what the speaker's real motive might be, and what selfish purpose he might not have hidden behind the mask of words. You find, for example, that an individual seeking to further his own petty and personal concerns, will block the advancement of an entire people.

---

72. Qur'án 59:9.

To turn his own water mill, he will let the farms and fields of all the others parch and wither. To maintain his own leadership, he will everlastingly direct the masses toward that prejudice and fanaticism which subvert the very base of civilization.

Such a man, at the same moment that he is 184 perpetrating actions which are anathema in the sight of God and detested by all the Prophets and Holy Ones, if he sees a person who has just finished eating wash his hands with soap—an article the inventor of which was 'Abdu'lláh Búní, a Muslim—will, because this unfortunate does not instead wipe his hands up and down the front of his robe and on his beard, set up a hue and cry to the effect that the religious law has been overthrown, and the manners and customs of heathen nations are being introduced into ours. Utterly disregarding the evil of his own ways, he considers the very cause of cleanliness and refinement as wicked and foolish.

O People of Persia! Open your eyes! Pay heed! 185 Release yourselves from this blind following of the bigots, this senseless imitation which is the principal reason why men fall away into paths of ignorance and degradation. See the true state of things. Rise up; seize hold of such means as will bring you life and happiness and greatness and glory among all the nations of the world.

186   The winds of the true springtide are passing over you; adorn yourselves with blossoms like trees in the scented garden. Spring clouds are streaming; then turn you fresh and verdant like the sweet eternal fields. The dawn star is shining, set your feet on the true path. The sea of might is swelling, hasten to the shores of high resolve and fortune. The pure water of life is welling up, why wear away your days in a desert of thirst? Aim high, choose noble ends; how long this lethargy, how long this negligence! Despair, both here and hereafter, is all you will gain from self-indulgence; abomination and misery are all you will harvest from fanaticism, from believing the foolish and the mindless. The confirmations of God are supporting you, the succor of God is at hand: why do you not cry out and exult with all your heart, and strive with all your soul!

Among those matters which require thorough revision and reform is the method of studying the various branches of knowledge and the organization of the academic curriculum. From lack of organization, education has become haphazard and confused. Trifling subjects which should not call for elaboration receive undue attention, to such an extent that students, over long periods of time, waste their minds and their energies on material that is pure supposition, in no way susceptible of proof, such study consisting in going deep into statements and concepts which careful examination would establish as not even unlikely, but rather as unalloyed superstition, and representing the investigation of useless conceits and the chasing of absurdities. There can be no doubt that to concern oneself with such illusions, to examine into and lengthily debate such idle propositions, is nothing but a waste of time and a marring of the days of one's life. Not only this, but it also prevents the individual from undertaking the study of those arts and sciences of which society stands in dire need. The individual should, prior to engaging in the study of any subject, ask himself what its uses are and what fruit and result will derive from it. If it is a useful branch of knowledge, that is, if society will gain important benefits from it, then he should certainly pursue it with all his heart. If not, if it consists in empty, profitless debates and in a vain concatenation of imaginings that lead to no result except acrimony, why devote one's life to such useless hairsplittings and disputes.

188   Because this matter requires further elucidation and a thorough hearing, so that it can be fully established that some of the subjects which today are neglected are extremely valuable, while the nation has no need whatever of various other, superfluous studies, the point will, God willing, be developed in a second volume. Our hope is that a reading of this first volume will produce fundamental changes in the thinking and the behavior of society, for We have undertaken the work with a sincere intent and purely for the sake of God. Although in this world individuals who are able to distinguish between sincere intentions and false words are as rare as the philosopher's stone, yet We fix Our hopes on the measureless bounties of the Lord.

To resume: As for that group who maintains   189
that in effecting these necessary reforms we must
proceed with deliberation, exercise patience and
gain the objectives one at a time, just what do
they mean by this? If by deliberation they are referring to that circumspection which the science
of government requires, their thought is timely
and appropriate. It is certain that momentous
undertakings cannot be brought to a successful
conclusion in haste; that in such cases haste would
only make waste.

The world of politics is like the world of man;   190
he is seed at first, and then passes by degrees to
the condition of embryo and foetus, acquiring a
bone structure, being clothed with flesh, taking
on his own special form, until at last he reaches
the plane where he can befittingly fulfill the words:
"the most excellent of Makers."[73] Just as this is a
requirement of creation and is based on the universal Wisdom, the political world in the same
way cannot instantaneously evolve from the na-

---

73. Qur'án 23:14: "Blessed therefore be God, the most
excellent of Makers."

dir of defectiveness to the zenith of rightness and perfection. Rather, qualified individuals must strive by day and by night, using all those means which will conduce to progress, until the government and the people develop along every line from day to day and even from moment to moment.

191 When, through the divine bestowals, three things appear on earth, this world of dust will come alive, and stand forth wondrously adorned and full of grace. These are first, the fruitful winds of spring; second, the welling plenty of spring clouds; and third, the heat of the bright sun. When, out of the endless bounty of God, these three have been vouchsafed, then slowly, by His leave, dry trees and branches turn fresh and green again, and array themselves with many kinds of blossoms and fruits. It is the same when the pure intentions and the justice of the ruler, the wisdom and consummate skill and statecraft of the governing authorities, and the determination and unstinted efforts of the people, are all combined; then day by day the effects of the advancement, of the far-reaching reforms, of the pride and prosperity of government and people alike, will become clearly manifest.

If, however, by delay and postponement they   192
mean this, that in each generation only one min-
ute section of the necessary reforms should be
attended to, this is nothing but lethargy and in-
ertia, and no results would be forthcoming from
such a procedure, except the endless repetition of
idle words. If haste is harmful, inertness and indolence are a thousand times worse. A middle
course is best, as it is written: "It is incumbent
upon you to do good between the two evils," this
referring to the mean between the two extremes.
"And let not thy hand be tied up to thy neck; nor
yet open it with all openness . . . but between these
follow a middle way."[74]

The primary, the most urgent requirement is   193
the promotion of education. It is inconceivable
that any nation should achieve prosperity and
success unless this paramount, this fundamental
concern is carried forward. The principal reason
for the decline and fall of peoples is ignorance.
Today the mass of the people are uninformed even
as to ordinary affairs, how much less do they grasp

---

74. Qur'án 17:31; 110.

the core of the important problems and complex needs of the time.

194　　It is therefore urgent that beneficial articles and books be written, clearly and definitely establishing what the present-day requirements of the people are, and what will conduce to the happiness and advancement of society. These should be published and spread throughout the nation, so that at least the leaders among the people should become, to some degree, awakened, and arise to exert themselves along those lines which will lead to their abiding honor. The publication of high thoughts is the dynamic power in the arteries of life; it is the very soul of the world. Thoughts are a boundless sea, and the effects and varying conditions of existence are as the separate forms and individual limits of the waves; not until the sea boils up will the waves rise and scatter their pearls of knowledge on the shore of life.

195　　*Thou, Brother, art thy thought alone,*
　　　The rest is only thew and bone.[75]

---

75. Rúmí, The *Mathnaví*, II 2:277. The next line is: A garden close, if that thought be a rose, But if it be a thorn, then only fit to burn.

Public opinion must be directed toward what-   196
ever is worthy of this day, and this is impossible
except through the use of adequate arguments and
the adducing of clear, comprehensive and conclusive proofs. For the helpless masses know nothing of the world, and while there is no doubt that
they seek and long for their own happiness, yet
ignorance like a heavy veil shuts them away from
it.

Observe to what a degree the lack of educa-   197
tion will weaken and degrade a people. Today
[1875] from the standpoint of population the
greatest nation in the world is China, which has
something over four hundred million inhabitants.
On this account, its government should be the
most distinguished on earth, its people the most
acclaimed. And yet on the contrary, because of
its lack of education in cultural and material civilization, it is the feeblest and the most helpless of
all weak nations. Not long ago, a small contingent of English and French troops went to war
with China and defeated that country so deci-
sively that they took over its capital Peking. Had
the Chinese government and people been abreast
of the advanced sciences of the day, had they been
skilled in the arts of civilization, then if all the

nations on earth had marched against them the attack would still have failed, and the attackers would have returned defeated whence they had come.

198   Stranger even than this episode is the fact that the government of Japan was in the beginning subject to and under the protection of China, and that now for some years, Japan has opened its eyes and adopted the techniques of contemporary progress and civilization, promoting sciences and industries of use to the public, and striving to the utmost of their power and competence until public opinion was focused on reform. This government has currently advanced to such a point that, although its population is only one-sixth, or even one-tenth, that of China, it has recently challenged the latter government, and China has finally been forced to come to terms. Observe carefully how education and the arts of civilization bring honor, prosperity, independence and freedom to a government and its people.

199   It is, furthermore, a vital necessity to establish schools throughout Persia, even in the smallest country towns and villages, and to encourage the people in every possible way to have their children learn to read and write. If necessary, educa-

tion should even be made compulsory. Until the
nerves and arteries of the nation stir into life, every measure that is attempted will prove vain; for
the people are as the human body, and determination and the will to struggle are as the soul,
and a soulless body does not move. This dynamic
power is present to a superlative degree in the very
nature of the Persian people, and the spread of
education will release it.

A s to that element who believe that it   200
is neither necessary nor appropriate
to borrow the principles of civilization,
the fundamentals of progress toward high levels
of social happiness in the material world, the
laws which effect thorough reforms, the methods
which extend the scope of culture—and that it
is far more suitable that Persia and the Persians
reflect over the situation and then create their
own techniques of progress.

It is certain that if the vigorous intelligence   201
and superior skill of the nation's great, and the

energy and resolve of the most eminent men at the imperial court, and the determined efforts of those who have knowledge and capacity, and are well versed in the great laws of political life, should all be combined, and all should exert every effort and examine and reflect over every detail as well as on the main currents of affairs, there is every likelihood that because of the effective plans they would evolve, some situations would be thoroughly reformed. In the majority of cases, however, they would still be obliged to borrow; because, throughout the many-centuried past, hundreds of thousands of persons have devoted their entire lives to putting these things to the test until they were able to bring about these substantial developments. If all that is to be ignored and an effort is made to re-create those agencies in our own country and in our own way, and thus effect the hoped-for advancement, many generations would pass by and still the goal would not be reached. Observe for instance that in other countries they persevered over a long period until finally they discovered the power of steam and by means of it were enabled easily to perform the heavy tasks which were once beyond human strength. How many centuries it would take if we were to abandon the use of this power and instead strain every nerve to invent a substitute. It is therefore preferable to keep on with the use of steam and at the same time continuously to examine into the possibility of there being a far greater force available. One should regard the other technological advances, sciences, arts and political formulae of proven usefulness in the same light— i.e., those procedures which, down the ages, have time and again been put to the test and whose many uses and advantages have demonstrably resulted in the glory and greatness of the state, and the well-being and progress of the people. Should all these be abandoned, for no valid reason, and other methods of reform be attempted, by the time such reforms might eventuate, and their advantages might be put to proof, many years would go by, and many lives. Meanwhile, "we are still at the first bend in the road."[76]

The superiority of the present in relation to the past consists in this, that the present can take 202

---

76. From the lines: "'Aṭṭár has passed through the seven cities of love, and we are still at the first bend in the road."

over and adopt as a model many things which have been tried and tested and the great benefits of which have been demonstrated in the past, and that it can make its own new discoveries and by these augment its valuable inheritance. It is clear, then, that the accomplishment and experience of the past are known and available to the present, while the discoveries peculiar to the present were unknown to the past. This presupposes that the later generation is made up of persons of ability; otherwise, how many a later generation has lacked even so much as a drop out of the boundless ocean of knowledge that was its forbears'.

203   Reflect a little: let us suppose that, through the power of God, certain individuals are placed on earth; these obviously stand in need of many things, to provide for their human dignity, their happiness and ease. Now is it more practicable for them to acquire these things from their contemporaries, or should they, in each successive generation, borrow nothing, but instead independently create one or another of the instrumentalities which are necessary to human existence?

204   Should some maintain that those laws, principles and fundamentals of progress on the highest levels of a fully developed society, which are

current in other countries, are not suited to the condition and the traditional needs of Persia's people, and that on this account it is necessary that within Írán, the nations' planners should exert their utmost efforts to bring about reforms appropriate to Persia—let them first explain what harm could come from such foreign importations.

If the country were built up, the roads repaired,   205 the lot of the helpless improved by various means, the poor rehabilitated, the masses set on the path to progress, the avenues of public wealth increased, the scope of education widened, the government properly organized, and the free exercise of the individual's rights, and the security of his person and property, his dignity and good name, assured—would all this be at odds with the character of the Persian people? Whatever is in conflict with these measures has already been proved injurious, in every country, and does not concern one locality more than another.

These superstitions result in their entirety   206 from lack of wisdom and understanding, and insufficient observation and analysis. Indeed, the majority of the reactionaries and the procrastinators are only concealing their own selfish interests under a barrage of idle words, and confusing the minds of the helpless masses with public statements which bear no relation to their well-concealed objectives.

207   O people of Persia! The heart is a divine trust; cleanse it from the stain of self-love, adorn it with the coronal of pure intent, until the sacred honor, the abiding greatness of this illustrious nation may shine out like the true morning in an auspicious heaven. This handful of days on earth will slip away like shadows and be over. Strive then that God may shed His grace upon you, that you may leave a favorable remembrance in the hearts and on the lips of those to come. "And grant that I be spoken of with honor by posterity."[77]

208   Happy the soul that shall forget his own good, and like the chosen ones of God, vie with his fellows in service to the good of all; until, strengthened by the blessings and perpetual confirmations of God, he shall be empowered to raise this mighty nation up to its ancient pinnacles of glory, and restore this withered land to sweet new life, and as a spiritual springtime, array those trees which are the lives of men with the fresh leaves, the blossoms and fruits of consecrated joy.

---

77. Qur'án 26:84.

Glossary

Abraham: Considered by Bahá'ís to be a Prophet, or Manifestation of God, He is also recognized as the founder of monotheism and the father of the Jewish and Arab peoples. Muḥammad, the Báb, and Bahá'u'lláh are among His descendants.

Abu'l-Fidá (1273–1331 A.D.): A historian and geographer whose two primary works were a history covering the pre-Islamic and Islamic periods up until 1329, *Mukhtasar ta'rikh al-bashar* ("Brief History of Man"), and a geography published in 1321 entitled *Taqwim al-buldan* ("Locating the Lands"). While both books were originally compiled by other authors, they were organized and augmented by Abu'l-Fidá. They were well-used resources for eighteenth- and nineteenth-century European Orientalists and were popular during the time of their publication in the Middle East.

Abú Sufyán: A Meccan merchant who tried a variety of means to silence Muḥammad, including attempting assassination, raiding the city Medina where Muḥammad resided, and playing a leading role in the Battle of the Confederates.

Once he realized that his efforts were bringing ill omens upon his tribesmen (the Quray<u>sh</u>), Abú Sufyán renounced polytheism in acceptance of the One True God and Muḥammad as the Apostle of God.

Alexander of Macedon (336–323 B.C.), also known as Alexander the Great: The king of Macedonia who overthrew the Persian Empire.

Andalusia: The southernmost region of Spain, bounded by the Mediterranean Sea on the southeast, the Atlantic Ocean on the southwest, and Portugal on the west, that flourished under Muslim rule from about 1086 to 1212 while the rest of Europe was still emerging from the Dark Ages.

Anú<u>sh</u>írván the Generous and the Just (d. 579 A.D.): Persian king who ruled the Sassanian empire from 531 to 579. He is remembered as a great reformer and patron of the arts and scholarship.

Arabian chronicles: Refers to *One Thousand and One Nights,* a collection of tales of unknown origin and authorship based in Central Asia.

Bahman son of Isfandíyár: Isfandíyár was a legendary hero from the Persian poet Ferdowsi's epic work entitled *Shahnameh* ("The Book of the Kings").

Battle of the Confederates: The Confederates were an assembly of Jewish leaders and tribes of the Quray<u>sh</u> who united in a pact to defeat Muḥammad in April of 627 A.D. After securing additional alliances from surrounding tribes, their army numbered ten thousand men. It was thought that their victory was secured by their sheer numbers alone and further guaranteed by Muḥammad's inability to secure the manpower and resources needed to defend Medina. But Muḥammad took the unusual advice of Salmán the Persian and managed to secure the city despite being outnumbered. The Battle of the Confederates was the last attempt of the Quraysh to defeat Muḥammad; Abú Sufyán led their retreat to Mecca, and the confederacy and its alliances dissolved.

Chaldea: Land in southern Iraq that borders the head of the Persian Gulf between the Arabian desert and the Euphrates delta.

Christ (c. 6–4 B.C.–30 A.D.): Recognized by Bahá'ís as a Manifestation of God and the founder of Christianity. The Bahá'í writings often refer to Christ as "the Spirit of God" and "the Son."

Cordova, Granada, Seville, Toledo: Provinces in Andalusia.

Emperor Constantine (February 27, c. 280–May 22, 337 A.D.), also known as Constantine the Great: The first Roman emperor to profess Christianity. He not only initiated the evolution of the empire into a Christian state but also provided the impulse for a distinctively Christian culture that prepared the way for the growth of Byzantine and Western medieval culture.

Exilarch ("Head of the Exile"): Refers to the leader of the Jews exiled from the kingdom of Judah to Babylon by Nebuchadnezzar II.

Ezra (4th century B.C.): Religious leader of the Jews who returned from exile in Babylon and reconstituted the Jewish community on the basis of the Torah.

Fátimid: Political and religious dynasty that dominated an empire in North Africa and subsequently in the Middle East from 909 to 1171 A.D.

Firaydún: A mythological king featured in Ferdowsi's epic poem *Shahnameh* ("The Book of the Kings"). According to legend, Firaydún defeated a tyrannical king and took leadership of the country for five hundred years. At the time of his death, his kingdom was divided among his three sons.

Franco-Prussian War (July 19, 1870–May 10, 1871): War between France and Prussia in which a coalition of German states led by Prussia defeated France.

Galen (129–c. 216 A.D.), also known as Galen of Pergamum: Greek physician, writer, and philosopher who exercised a dominant influence on medical theory and practice in Europe from the Middle Ages until the mid-seventeenth century. His authority in the Byzantine world and the Muslim Middle East was similarly long lived.

Gulpáygán: A town in west-central Iran.

Hájí Mírzá Áqásí (c. 1783–1849): Grand Vizier of Persia whose cruelty, treachery, and misrule brought the country to the edge of ruin.

Hegira: The flight of Muḥammad from Mecca to Medina in 622 A.D. The first year of the Muslim calendar is taken to be the year of the Hegira.

Hezekiah: Thirteenth successor of David as King of Jerusalem who ruled during the late eighth and early seventh centuries B.C.

Ḥijáz (Hejaz): A region in northwest Saudi Arabia that is perhaps best known for the Islamic holy city of Mecca, which lies within it.

Holy Tradition (Ḥadíth): An oral tradition, later recorded in written form, associated with the recorded sayings of the Prophet Muḥammad. As a source of moral guidance, it is second only to the authority of the Qur'án.

Hulágú Khán (c. 1217–1265): Mongol ruler in Iran and a grandson of Genghis Khan who subdued the Islamic world.

Imám Riḍá: Eighth imam of the Twelver Shí'ihs who was appointed as successor to the caliph al-Ma'mún in an attempt to heal the division between the Sunnís and the Shí'ihs.

Magians or Magi: A caste of Zoroastrian priests and sages among the ancient Persians.

Mecca: Birthplace of Muḥammad and site of pilgrimage for Muslims today.

Medina or **Al-Medina:** Literally *the city,* so called as giving shelter to Muḥammad, known in ancient times as Yathrib. The burial place of Muḥammad; second only to Mecca in its sanctity to Muslims.

Mesopotamia: Region in southwestern Asia where the world's earliest civilization developed. The name comes from a Greek word meaning "between rivers," referring to the land between the Tigris and Euphrates rivers, but the region can be broadly defined to include the area that is now eastern Syria, southeastern Turkey, and most of Iraq.

Muḥammad (570–632 A.D.): The Prophet and Founder of Islam. Bahá'ís regard Muḥammad as a Manifestation of God and His book, the Qur'án, as holy scripture.

Mujtahid: A learned scholar of Islam deemed knowledge-able enough to interpret religious law.

Nebuchadnezzar (reigned c. 1119–c. 1098 B.C.): Babylonian king who destroyed Jerusalem during his reign.

Peking: Beijing.

Pentateuch: Literally *the fivefold volume;* refers to the first five books of the Old Testament. Known also as the Torah.

People of the Book, *Ahl al-Kitab:* This Islamic expression refers to religions such as Judaism, Christianity, and Zoro-astrianism, whose adherents seek guidance from divinely-inspired books (the Torah, the Gospel, the Avesta) as op-posed to religions not based on divine revelation. Muḥammad extended many privileges to People of the Book which were not extended to heathens.

Píshdádíyán Dynasty: A legendary dynasty of Iran, illustrated in Ferdowsi's epic Persian poem, *Shahnameh* ("The Book of the Kings").

Prophet of God: Designation of a Prophet Who is the Founder of a religious Dispensation, inasmuch as in His words, His person, and His actions He manifests the nature and purpose of God in accordance with the capacity and needs of the people to whom He comes.

Qur'án or **Koran:** The holy scripture of Islám, revealed by Muḥammad in Arabic.

Quraysh: The ruling tribe of Mecca into which Muḥammad was born. The Quraysh controlled west coast trade routes on the Arabian peninsula, which afforded them considerable influence.

Saladin (c. 1137/38–March 4, 1193): Muslim sultan of Egypt, Syria, Yemen, and Palestine, founder of the Ayyubid dynasty, and the most famous of Muslim heroes. In wars against the Christian Crusaders, he achieved great success with the capture of Jerusalem (Oct. 2, 1187), ending its nearly nine decades of occupation by the Franks.

Saljúqs: Ruling military family of one of the Turkmen tribes that invaded southwestern Asia in the eleventh century and eventually founded an empire that included Mesopotamia, Syria, Palestine, and most of Iran.

Salmán the Persian: A follower of Muḥammad who presented an unusual scheme during the Battle of the Confederates, which secured the safety of the city Medina. During the months of Ramaḍán (fasting), Salmán the Persian suggested that Muḥammad's followers dig a deep moat around the city. When the four-thousand-man Confederate army arrived, their camels and horses were unable to advance past the moat, and the soldiers who entered the trench were shot by archers on the opposite side.

Sea of Marmara: Inland sea partly separating the Asiatic and European parts of Turkey. It is connected through the Bosporus on the northeast with the Black Sea and through the Dardanelles on the southwest with the Aegean Sea.

Solomon (10th century B.C.): A son of David; generally regarded as the greatest king of Israel.

Sun of Truth: God, or His Manifestation, depending upon the context.

Tamerlane (1336–1405 A.D.): Turkish conqueror of Islamic territories in India, Russia, and the Mediterranean area.

Titus (39–91 A.D.): Roman emperor and the conqueror of Jerusalem in 70 A.D.

Tradition(s): The authoritative record of inspired sayings and acts of the Prophet, in addition to the revelation contained in the Qur'án.

'Ulamá: From the Arabic *'alima,* "to know"; may be translated as "learned men," "scientists," or "religious authorities."

Universal Manifestation: A Prophet of God, a divinely inspired Founder of a religious Dispensation, often referred to as a Manifestation of God, Whose appearance during a universal cycle causes the world to attain to maturity, and the extension of Whose cycle is very great. Afterward other Manifestations will arise under His shadow. Bahá'u'lláh is the Universal Manifestation for the current universal cycle.

Yathrib (Medina): City located in the Ḥijáz region of western Saudi Arabia, about one hundred miles (160 kilometers) inland from the Red Sea and 275 miles from Mecca by road. It is one of Islám's two holiest cities, with Mecca being the other.

Index

Note: index locators refer to paragraph numbers.

A

Abraham
  laws of, 52
Alexander of Macedon
  Conqueror on three continents, 125
Algebra
  Acquired from Greeks, 54, 54n21
America
  Civilization renowned, 19
Ammon
  Israelites settled, 142
Andalusia
  Europe learned sciences from, 161
Anger
  Master it; Qur'án, 167
Anúshírván the Generous Persian king (531–578 A.D.)
  just, 126

Arabia
    Civilization due to Muḥammad, 9, 158, 160
    Conquests of nations, 159, 162
    Sciences, arts, excelled in, 158, 160–62
    Uncivilized practices, 158–59
Arabs
    Pagan, observed truces, 49n17
Armaments
    Limited by law, should be, 120

B

Báb and Bahá'u'lláh
    Foretold in Matthew 24:36, 99n36
Babylon
    Capture of Israelites, 143
Backbiting
    Harmful to faith of masses, 101
Believers
    Requirements, 59–65
Books
    Persia urgently needs, 195

C

Caliphs
    Fátimid, ruled Egypt, Syria, 161
Canaan
    Israel's homeland, 140

Capital punishment
    Control of needed in Persia, 178
Catholic Church
    Voltaire attached, 132
Character
    Christians transformed, 154
    Good, most praiseworthy all things, 108
    Moderation, basis of, 108
Charity
    Christians practiced, 154
Children
    Lawless, need education, 171
China
    Degraded by lack education, 198
    Rejected of God, idol worship, 47
Christianity
    Crusades, 162
    Middle Ages, worldly, corrupt, 157
    Propagation by holy deeds, 81
    Protestantism growing, 77–78
    Story of Nu'mán, 83–95
Christians
    Educational institutions founded, 155
    Galen promised morals of, 151
    People of the Book; Qur'án, 47
    Tortured, 81
    Transformed world, 148
Civilization
    Based on: justice, 6, 120–26; power of intellect, 1–5;
            religion, 131
    Destroyed by: fanaticism, prejudice, 183
    Education leads to, 182

Civilization *(continued)*
    External, useless, 109
    Objective human well-being, 109
    Persia could develop perfect, 8
    Spiritually learned aid, 59
    Virtues of; Qur'án, 167
Clergy
    Spirituality of not universal, 106
Compassion
    Attribute of perfection, 74
Conquest
    Praiseworthy at times, 129
Conscience
    Pray for development of, 4
Constantine, Emperor
    Established Roman justice, mercy, 154
Consultation
    Bedrock of government, 31
    Encouraged by Qur'án, 176
Courage
    Attribute of perfection, 74
Courts
    Deviation from spiritual law, 34
    Written code essential for, 68–70
Creation
    Primacy of intellect and wisdom in, 1
Criticism
    Harmful to spirituality, 101
Crusades
    European civilization dates from, 162
Cyrus, King of Persia
    Ruler of all ancient world, 13

D

Day of Resurrection
    Book wide open; Qur'án, 180
Days of Ignorance
    Customs of, retained by Muḥammad, 49–51
    Paganism in Arabia, 51
    Story: Day of Evil, Day of Grace, 83–95
Defender of the Faith
    Meaning of, 75
Desire
    "Blot out virtue" poem, 119
    "Devouring fire" eats up character, 108
Devotion
    Not relevant to outer appearance, 106
Divine Law (*see also* Law)
    Purpose in revelation of, 106
    Revelation of by Muḥammad, 49–52
Divine Law-Giver
    Reforms not contrary to laws of, 47
Divines
    Encourage learning, civilization of, 46
    Lamps of guidance, physicians, 59
Draper, John William
    The Intellectual Development of Europe, 164–65

E

Edom
    Israelites settled, 142

Education
Compulsory, 200
Lack of, weakens, degrades, 198
Masses, highest righteousness, 182
Must be organized, useful, 188
Needed by mankind, 72, 171
Persian leaders neglect, 180
Prosperity depends on, 193
Egypt
Islám ruled, 162
Israelites in, 142
Europe
Civilization due to knowledge, 19
Civilization superficial, immoral, 109–18
The Intellectual Development of Europe by Draper, 164–65
Islám, civilization, laws of, preserved in libraries, 161–65
Middle Ages, barbaric, 157
Morally uncivilized, 109–18
War plans, 112–18
Evil
Indolence, lethargy, 192
Prejudice, fanaticism, 183
Ezra
Established Divine Law, 142

F

Faith
Belief put to proof; Qur'án, 48
Lack of, cause of injustice, oppression, 34

Promises rewards hereafter, 170
Story of Nu'mán, 83–95
Unselfish service, fosters, 170
Fanaticism
Causes backbiting, 101
Hindrance to others, 98
Repulses friendships, 101
Subverts civilization, 183
Fate
Fastened about man's neck, 181
Firaydún, King of Persia
Ruler of ancient world, 13
Fitzgerald, Edward
Rubaiyat, quote from, 95n31
Forbearance
Attribute of perfection, 74
Foreigners
Borrowing knowledge, etc. from, permissible, 53–59
Fellowship with, leads to faith, 99
Muḥammad borrowed customs from, 49–52
France
Wars with Germany, 115–118
Franco-Prussian War
Destructiveness of, 115
Future
Bright, depends upon justice, kindness, 124

G

Galen
Christians, praised morals, 152

Generosity
    Attribute of perfection, 74
    Wealth disbursed to needy, 167
Germany
    Religious hostilities, 116
    Wars with France, 115–18
God
    Emblem of intellect, 2–5
    Fear of, 73–74
    Love of, 10, 73–74
    Nearness to, human happiness, 109
    Obedience to, man's glory, 130
Government
    Justice protects human rights, 25
    Legislators need religion, education, 31–34
    Sincerity of, 43
    Wisdom, justice two banners of, 127
Greeks
    Received philosophy from Israel, 141
Guns
    Use of most modern, 56

H

Ḥájí Mírzá Áqásí
    Prime Minister of Persia, 177
Happiness
    Aim of mankind, 5
    Closeness to God, 109
    Due to high endeavors, 6
    Masses veiled from by ignorance, 196

Means to, qualities, 109
Obedience to laws of Holy Books, 130
Objective of civilization, 109
Religion, basis of, 174
Heart
Divine trust, 207
"Divinely kindled fire" of, 4
Hermits
Spiritual idleness, 73
Hezekiah
Reestablished Divine Law, 142
Ḥijáz
People of, brutish before Muḥammad, 158
Holy Ones
Station of, 38
Honor
Attribute of perfection, 74
Hulágú Khán
Conqueror of Asia, 125
Humanity
Oneness of, 71

I

Idleness
Condemned, not spiritual, 73
Ignorance
Barbaric, 6
Causes savagery, wretchedness, 7
Imitation
Causes degradation, 185
Foreign nations, Qur'án encourages, 175

Independence
    Not due to appearance, 106
Industries
    Persia needs, 179
Injustice
    Caused by lack of faith, 34
Instinct
    Not source of uprightness, 171
Intellect
    Emblem of God, first, 2
    Power of, 2–5
Islám
    Asleep; must awake, 80
    Confession of faith, 99n
    Draper, *The Intellectual Development of Europe,* 164–65
    Europe learned sciences from, 161–62
    Obedience to could convert world, 76–82
    Rose to heights of learning, 9
    Spain, civilization under, 165
    Sword, propagated by, falsehood, 80
Israelites
    Civilization based on religion, 140
    Decline from religion, 142
    Dispersion after Roman conquest, 142
    Egypt, enslavement in, 142
    Jesus, persecuted, lost power, 145–49
    Noble attributes, 140
    Praised for virtues, 140
    Prophecies of punishment; Qur'án, 142

J

Japan
    Progressive, greater than China, 198
Jericho
    Israelites settled, 142
Jeroboam
    Introduced worship of idols, 142
Jerusalem
    Sacked by Titus, 142
Jesus
    Conferred eternal life, 144
    Disciples martyred, 81
    Divine Revelation, remedy for the world, 81
    Ministry, teachings of, 144–46
    Righteousness, basis of civilization, 145
Jews
    Persecuted Jesus, 145–46
Jordan
    Israelites settled, 142
Justice
    Dependent upon sincerity of elected representatives, 43
    Impartial obedience to law, 71
    Necessary for peace, 124–27
    Power of, invincible, 127
    Religion commands; Qur'án, 167
    Rights of others preserved, 74
    Written code essential for, 69–70

K

Kings
Just, station high, 38
Knowledge
Causes social good, 5
Is happiness, 5
Light in heart; Qur'án, 59
Nation's pride, 5
Pearls on shore of life, 194
Progress needs, 104
Standards of, 75–82

L

Law (*see also* Divine Law)
Abraham, 52
Establish in cities, 179
European derived from Muslims, 161, 165
God's
Death sentence conditional, 177
Despotism contrary to, 178
Elected leaders must be cognizant of, 31
Instrument of education, 150
Happiness and obedience to, 130
Highest principles of, 31
Integrity and equality of persons, 25
Jesus Christ, 81, 146
Mosaic, 142
Muḥammad revealed, 49–52
Political, 166–67
Religious, 69
Searching out implications of, 75–76

Laymen
    Spirituality of, surpass clergy, 106
Leaders
    Awakened through education, 194
    Moral integrity needed, 35
Learned persons
    Qualifications of, 59–184
        Defend one's faith, 62, 71–106
        Guard one's own self, 62–70
        Obey the commandments of the Lord, 62,
           129–84
        Oppose one's passions, 62,
           107–29
Learning
    Attribute, first, of perfection, 64
Lethargy
    Condemned, 163, 186
Litigations
    Written law essential for, 69–70
Logic
    Founder of Sabean, 54
Love
    Attribute of perfection, 74
    Enemies, 146
    Fellowship, based on religion, 135
    God, by acquiring perfections, 74
    God, source of virtues, 167
    Self, inherent in man, 170
Loyalty
    Attribute of perfection, 74
Luther, Martin
    Protestant reforms correct, 77

M

Man
  Not puny, 36
Mankind
  Educator, needs, 171
  Excellence due to mind, 5–6
  Intellect first endowment, 2
  Wretchedness due to base appetites, 4
Masses
  Education of, highest righteousness, 182
  Ignorance veils from happiness, 196
Mecca
  Muḥammad lit lamp of, 158
Medina (Yathrib)
  Enlightened by Muḥammad, 158
Middle Ages
  Christianity declined, 157
  Europe dark, 19
Mind
  Created first by God, 2
Ministers of state
  Station high if wise, honest, 39–42
Monasticism
  Spiritual idleness, 73
Muḥammad
  Borrowed customs from Persia, 48
  Civilization, renewed, 9, 158–62
  Gentle, long-suffering; Qur'án, 98
  King of Anúshírván, praised by, 126
  Law of, retained some ancient customs, 48–52
  Proofs of Prophethood, 160

Prophet by the sword untrue, 80
Sciences, arts, encourages, 175

N

Napoleon I
Conqueror of three continents, 125
Futile life, 125
Nation (or state)
Based on legislative and executive forces, 67
Nations
Borrow sciences from each other, 57
Nature
Ignorant, needs education, 171
Nebuchadnezzar
King of Babylon, captured Israelites, 142
Negroes
African, converted to Protestantism, 77
Nu'mán
Story: Day of Evil, Day of Grace, 83–95

P

Parliaments
Elected, increases justice, 43
Must be God-fearing, incorruptible, 31
Qur'án encourages, 176
Passions
Oppose, 107–8

Patience
    Under hardships, 167
Peace
    Achievement of, 121–22
    Covenant, establish, 120–22
    Force cannot bring, 112
    Universal, means to, 120–22, 129
Pentateuch (Torah)
    Laws of Abraham, contains, 52
    Tampered with, 52
People
    Enlightened, 58–65
Perfection
    Attributes of, 64–74
    Nothing to do with appearance, 106
    Religion source of, 167
Persia
    Ancient civilization, noble, 8
    Army, needs reform, 27–28
    Bigots, cause of degradation, 185
    Books, publications, needed, 194
    Bribery, should be abolished, 27
    Corruption, 15, 27–28
    Culture, education, neglected, 180–87
    Decadence, 15–17
    Foreign relations, recommended, 26
    Future depends on education, 8, 207–8
    Government: despotic, 177–78; first on earth, 14; local,
        corrupt, 27–28
    History of, learning, power, 12–17
    Ignorance widespread, 5–6, 15
    Justice hampered by ignorance, 34
    Muḥammad borrowed customs from, 48

Past glory quenched, 163

People of: innate, intelligence, 18; ignorant, irreligious, 33

Population depleted by wars, killing, 178

Progress: blind to need for, 180; depends on leaders, 201–8

Public opinion, disunited, 28

Reforms censured by ignorant, 21–35

Rich in natural resources, 18

Schools must multiply, 197–99

Sciences, needed from foreign countries, 201–7

Sháh: blamed for reforms, 20; encourages justice, education, 10, 20; influenced by God, 20, urged to strive for regeneration, 186

Philistia
 Israel's homeland, 140

Philosophers
 Christians, compared to, 152–53

Phoenicia
 Israelites settled, 142

Physician
 Wise needed, 174

Police force
 Internal scrutiny, 121

Politics
 Reform, needed, 190–92

Popes
 Crusades, 192
 Gerbert, educated in Spain, 165
 Power in Europe 1500 A.D., 77

Power
 Intellect of man, 3
 Latent in human effort, 122

Prejudice
    Subverts civilization, 185
Priests
    Sometimes veil religion, 170
Progress
    Built on knowledge of past, 201–5
    Pure intention promotes, 8
Prophets
    Civilizations brought by, 167–75
Prosperity
    Education greatest aid to, 193
Protestant Churches
    Activities, extension of, 77–78
Purity
    Not relevant to outer appearance, 106
Pythagoras
    Greek philosopher, learned from Israelites, 141

R

Reality of man
    Intellect, wisdom, 1–5
Reforms
    Education in, 187–89
    Foreign importations, praiseworthy, 47–58
Rehoboam
    Son of Solomon, 142
Rejection
    Effect on strangers, 99

Religion
  Agency for unity, agreement, 135
  Basis of culture, civilization, 138–55
  Defend and propagate, 75–82
  Educator in love, morals, 150–55
  Happiness, brings, 131–74
  Judge by principles, 131
  Light of world, 130
  Nature, reinforces, 173
  Obstacle to progress untrue, 131
  Propagate by perfections, not sword, 82
  Purpose: happiness, character, 82
  Source of: civilizations, virtues, 166–75; sacrifice,
      unselfishness, 170
  Virtues, teaches, 173
Religions
  Associate kindly with all, 99
Religious leaders (*see* Divines)
Resurrection (*see* Day of Resurrection)
Revelation
  Influence on civilization, 159
Righteousness
  Defined; Qur'án, 167
  Education of masses, 182
  Guidance toward, righteous act, 10
  Natural, reinforced by religion, 173
Rome
  Conquest of Israelites, 142
Rúmí, Jalálu'ddín
  Mathnaví, 61, 133, 137, 195, 195n75

S

Saladin
  Conquered Egypt, Syria, 162
Salvation
  Obedience to Lord, 130
Schools
  Persia in urgent need of, 193–99
Science
  Develops civilizations; not contrary to religion, 179
  Emanations of mind, 5
  Progresses age after age, 201–5
  Raises man to excellence, 25
  Society stands in dire need, 187
Scientists
  Station high, praiseworthy, 40
Scriptures
  Source of civilization, 168
Selfishness
  Contemptible, 7
  Criticism of others related to, 101–2
Self-love
  Kneaded into man, 170
Servants of God
  Oneness of, 71
Service
  Common good, noblest, 182
  Man's faculties bestowed for, 5
S̲h̲áh of Írán (see Persia)
Sin
  Blocks progress, 182–83
  Indolence, lethargy, 192

Sincerity
    Attribute of perfection, 74
    Foundation of faith, 170
Socrates
    Learned from Israelites, 141
Soap
    Invented by a Muslim, 184
Spain
    Civil War, 116
    Islamic civilization, schools, 165
Spirituality
    Aids others, brings progress, 104–6
    Foundation of: oppose passions, 107–8
    Idleness condemned, 73
    Qualities, 59–65, 98–101
Statesmen
    Called to account, 180
    Rank next to just kings, 39–42
Superstition
    Veils from true knowledge, 187
Sword
    Reject as means propagate faith, 80–82
Syria
    Ruled by Islám, 162
    Saladin captured, 162

T

Tamerlane
    Conqueror of Asia, 125
    Futile life, 125

Teaching
    Associate with all faiths, 99
    Duty every believer, 81
    Gentleness, 98
    Knowledge other religions necessary, 64–66
Titus
    Roman conqueror of Israel, 142
Torah (*see* Pentateuch)
Trustworthiness
    Attribute of perfection, 74

U

'Ulamá
    Arbitrary judges, 69
Unity
    Based on religion, 135
    God source of, 136–37
Universal peace (*see* Peace)
Unselfishness
    Religion gives power for, 170

V

Virtues
    Attract souls, 99–100
    Civilized; Qur'án, 167
    Desire blots out (poem), 119
    Middle way between two evils, 192
    Named, 74

Serving the masses, 182
Wisdom and justice, most potent, 127
Voltaire
Attacked religion, 132–38
Reasoning unsound, 132

W

War
Abolish, how to, 120–21
Cost borne by people, 113
Destruction of happiness, 114
Europe's preparations for, 111
Intolerable, will become, 123
Modern weapons needed, 56
Muḥammad borrowed moat from Persians, 48
Righteous, 129
Weapons, sapping wealth, 112–18
Wealth
Praiseworthy used for public good, 46
Weapons
Cost borne by people, 113
Wicked
Misled, 134
Wisdom
Invincible, 127
Reality of man, 1–8
Words
Insufficient, deeds necessary, 173
World
Benefits of relatively insignificant, 170
Envy of worlds of light, 3

World *(continued)*
    Progress of, 6
    Revivication of, 191

Bahá'í
PUBLISHING
and the Bahá'í Faith

Bahá'í Publishing produces books based on the teachings of the Bahá'í Faith. Founded more than 160 years ago, the Bahá'í Faith has spread to some 235 nations and territories and is now accepted by more than five and a half million people. The word "Bahá'í" means "follower of Bahá'u'lláh." Bahá-u'lláh, the founder of the Bahá'í Faith, asserted that he is the Messenger of God for all of humanity in this day. The cornerstone of his teachings is the establishment of the spiritual unity of humankind, which will be achieved by personal transformation and the application of clearly identified spiritual principles. Bahá'ís also believe that there is but one religion and that all the Messengers of God—among them Abraham, Zoroaster, Moses, Krishna, Buddha, Jesus, and Muḥammad—have progressively revealed its nature. Together, the world's great religions are expressions of a single, unfolding divine plan. Human beings, not God's Messengers, are the source of religious divisions, prejudices, and hatreds.

The Bahá'í Faith is not a sect or denomination of another religion, nor is it a cult or a social movement. Rather, it is a globally recognized independent world religion founded on new books of scripture revealed by Bahá'u'lláh.

Bahá'í Publishing is an imprint of the National Spiritual Assembly of the Bahá'ís of the United States.

For more information about the Bahá'í Faith,
or to contact the Bahá'ís near you, visit
http://www.bahai.us/
or call
1-800-22-UNITE

Other Books Available from Bahá'í Publishing

The Ascent of Society
The Social Imperative in Personal Salvation
John S. Hatcher
$19.95 U.S. / $22.95 CAN
Trade Paper
1-931847-52-5
978-1-931847-52-0

An illuminating examination of the relationship between individual spiritual development and the collective advancement of civilization.

In *The Purpose of Physical Reality* Dr. John S. Hatcher compared the physical world to a classroom designed by God to stimulate individual spiritual growth and to prepare us for birth into a spiritual existence. But how does personal spiritual development translate into social experience? Is there a social imperative connected with individual spiritual growth? Is involvement with others necessary for one to evolve spiritually? Hatcher analyzes these questions and more in *The Ascent of Society: The Social Imperative in Personal Salvation*. This penetrating study describes the objective of personal spiritual growth as an "ever-expanding sense of self" that requires social relationships in order to develop. Hatcher focuses on the Bahá'í belief that human history is a divinely guided process in which spiritual principles are gradually and progressively expressed in social institutions. He demonstrates that the aspirant to spiritual transformation cannot view personal health and development as being possible apart from the progress of human society as a whole.

John S. Hatcher holds a BA and MA in English literature from Vanderbilt University and a PhD in English literature from the University of Georgia. He is the director of graduate studies in English literature at the University of South Florida, Tampa. A widely published poet and distinguished lecturer, he has written numerous books on literature, philosophy, and Bahá'í theology and scripture, including *Close Connections: The Bridge between Spiritual and Physical Reality, From the Auroral Darkness: The Life and Poetry of Robert E. Hayden, A Sense of History: The Poetry of John Hatcher, The Ocean of His Words: A Reader's Guide to the Art of Bahá'u'lláh,* and *The Purpose of Physical Reality.* He and his family live on a farm near Plant City, Florida.

Hidden Gifts
Finding Blessings in the Struggles of Life
Brian Kurzius
$10.95 U.S. / $13.95 CAN
Trade Paper
1-931847-48-7
978-1-931847-48-3

Have you ever wondered why we have problems and tests in our lives? Where do they come from? What is the most effective way to handle them? We may not see it, but there just might be a multitude of gifts hidden among our problems and tests.

In *Hidden Gifts: Finding Blessings in the Struggles of Life*, author Brian Kurzius searches the Bahá'í scriptures for answers to the meaning of human suffering. What is the value of suffering in our lives? How do we decide on the best course of action? Are there qualities and attributes we can develop to help us more effectively face life's challenges? The answers to these questions and others are found in this spiritually edifying collection of extracts from Bahá'í scripture.

Over the course of many years, author Brian Kurzius has studied the subject of human suffering extensively. His research increasingly drew him to the writings of the Bahá'í Faith on the subject. He now offers workshops and lectures frequently about finding gifts in the struggles of life. Kurzius is also the author of *Fire & Gold: Benefitting from Life's Tests*. Brian and his wife, Christine, live in Haifa, Israel, where they work for the Bahá'í World Center.

Religion on the Healing Edge
What Bahá'ís Believe
Frank Stetzer
$11.95 U.S. / $14.95 CAN
Trade Paper
1-931847-44-4
978-1-931847-44-5

An introduction to the Bahá'í Faith that challenges readers to view religion, civilization, and spirituality in a new way.

Religion on the Healing Edge: What Bahá'ís Believe examines the defining beliefs animating the Bahá'í Faith and its distinctive practices, which are intended to change the world. Author Frank Stetzer offers insights into the Bahá'í community and its vision to establish a new global civilization based on the recognition of the oneness of humanity. The vision he presents is a bold and audacious one, full of unique opportunities and unusual challenges. A marvelous book for anyone interested in learning more about the mission of the Bahá'í Faith and the relevance of its teachings.

Frank Stetzer is a research statistician in the College of Nursing at the University of Wisconsin-Milwaukee. He holds a PhD in geography and an MS in statistics from the University of Iowa. Dr. Stetzer encountered the Bahá'í religion as a college student in the 1970s. He and his wife, Rosemary, have served in various capacities in several Bahá'í communities. They live in Wisconsin and enjoy the company of their three children.

A Way out of the Trap
A Ten-Step Program for Spiritual Growth
Nathan Rutstein
$10.95 U.S. / $13.95 CAN
Trade Paper
1-931847-40-1
978-1-931847-40-7

An easy-to-follow guide for people of all faiths to reconnect with God and live more fulfilling lives.

A Way Out of the Trap: A Ten-Step Program for Spiritual Growth offers a process by which the spiritually hungry can find the faith, hope, and spiritual sustenance needed to break out of the trap of hopelessness. Author Nathan Rutstein outlines a spiritual path that can help people of all faiths to reconnect with God. The result is a practical guide to understanding the purpose of life and how to live it.

Author, lecturer, college educator, and former network journalist, Nathan Rutstein has written numerous books about life, spirituality, racism, education, and the oneness of humanity. He is also one of the founders of the Institute for the Healing of Racism in the United States, lecturing at scores of colleges, universities and government institutions on the subject.